James Hill Fitts

Genealogy of the Fitts Or Fitz Family in America

Salzwasser

James Hill Fitts

Genealogy of the Fitts Or Fitz Family in America

1. Auflage | ISBN: 978-3-84605-062-0

Erscheinungsort: Frankfurt, Deutschland

Erscheinungsjahr: 2020

Salzwasser Verlag GmbH

Reprint of the original, first published in 1869.

GENEALOGY

OF THE

FITTS OR FITZ FAMILY

IN AMERICA,

— BY —

JAMES HILL FITTS,

RESIDENT MEMBER OF THE

New England Historic - Genealogical Society.

CLINTON:
PRINTED BY WM. J. COULTER.
COURANT OFFICE.

GENEALOGY

OF THE

FITTS OR FITZ FAMILY

IN AMERICA,

— BY —

JAMES HILL FITTS,

RESIDENT MEMBER OF THE

New England Historic - Genealogical Society.

CLINTON:
PRINTED BY WM. J. COULTER.
COURANT OFFICE.
1869.

PREFACE.

THIS book is the fruit of many years of extended investigation and patient research. Those only who have engaged in similar pursuits can be aware of the untold labor required to collect and systematize the jumbled materials for a volume like this. The driblets have been culled here and there from state, county, town, parish, church and family records, and from an extended correspondence with individuals who were intimately connected with particular branches of the family. To the many valued friends who have assisted in the enterprize grateful acknowledgments are tendered.

It is confidently felt that while unimportant inaccuracies may appear, the genealogy as a whole is perfectly reliable. This assertion is made in full view of the consideration that many persons who will peruse these pages have much better means of information concerning some families than can reasonably be expected from the writer. Those who are competent to detect blemishes will, it is hoped, make due allowance should they be found, while they remember it is much easier to find fault with the work than to do it better. It is well nigh impossible to produce a publication of this kind which shall be entirely free from imperfections. A certain author defines all history to be merely "an approximation towards truth." Without endorsing fully this humiliating statement, yet, when the imperfection of everything human is considered, it must be admitted the sentiment has some foundation in fact. There doubtless are omissions in the book though it includes, so far as could be obtained, every person of the name in its varied orthography throughout the United States. And there are probably some mistakes since it is impossible at this late day to prepare genealogical statistics with perfect accuracy. Honest George Dyer, a classical scholar and writer of the last generation whose long life of literary toil exemplified the extreme care he eulogizes, asks enthusiastically, "Who can calculate on the consequence of a *single date*, sometimes to an individual, sometimes to a family, and sometimes even to the public ?" If under the circumstances, the depravity of figures has represented some individuals as born a century or two out of time, or forced them into incongruous marriages, or prematurely consigned them to the shades, they can console themselves with the reflection that they are at liberty still to live on as though no such mishap had occurred.

Very few such books will ever be written a second time ; the pains are too great and the praise is too little. In the present instance however, the "years and years of dismal drudgery evidenced upon every page " has been a labor of love. The annalist designs the present issue only as the foundation of a volume yet more extended and complete to be put to press at some day in the near future. This will afford opportunity to correct any mistakes which may have inadvertently crept into the present text, and also for additions in the form of extended notices of distinguished members of the family, thereby greatly enhancing the interest and value of the forthcoming work. Massive materials of this kind are already on hand which can be arranged for the press in a comparatively short time if sufficient encouragement shall be afforded to warrant the undertaking. A manuscript is already completed containing the genealogy of Sir John Fitz of Fitz–ford, Devonshire County, England, embracing five generations in the 13th and 14th centuries. And there is little or no doubt that this is the ancient source of the family in America.

No apology is needed for such an undertaking as this ; it justifies itself. It cannot but afford satisfaction to know that some of the old Puritan blood flows in our veins. Unquestionably they were the most remarkable body of men which the world has ever produced. To this noble ancestry we owe a deep debt of esteem and gratitude we can never fully repay.

> " They that on glorious ancestors enlarge,
> Prove their debt, instead of their discharge."
>
> *Night Thoughts.*

We may heed Cowper's caution and do something toward discharging our indebtedness by bringing from the treasures of the past and holding up to the view of the present and of coming generations, their example of private virtue and of public usefulness ; their self-denying moderation in counsel and unsparing energy in action ; and, above all, their childlike trust in God, and their implicit faith in the Gospel of Christ as the only sure foundation of Christian churches, schools and institutions.

West Boylston, Mass.

CONTENTS.

	PAGE.
PREFACE,	V
THE FAMILY IN THE UNITED STATES,	1
NEW HAMPSHIRE BRANCH,	5
ESSEX COUNTY BRANCH,	31
BRISTOL COUNTY BRANCH,	42
WORCESTER COUNTY BRANCH,	50
MAINE BRANCH,	76
INDEX OF CHRISTIAN NAMES,	79
NAMES OF COLLATERAL FAMILIES,	87

The Family in the United States.

The American ancestor of the family of FITTS or FITZ, was ROBERT, who, with his wife, GRACE D., was among the original settlers of Salisbury, Mass.

" At a Generall Court held at Boston, the 6th day of the 7th month, 1638, Mr. Bradstreet and associates are alowed (vpon their petition) to begin a plantation at Merrimack." In 1639, Winthrop says that another plantation was begun upon the north side of Merrimack, called Salisbury.

The record of land granted Robert Fitts is on page 21 of the early town records. "The first or original list of yᵉ townsmen of Salisbury in yᵉ booke of Records.

Rob. ffitts.   [68 in all.]

This is a true copie as they were first listed in yᵉ booke of Records. As attests ;   Tho. Bradbury, rec'r."

The name " Robert Fitt, Planter," as he signed it, occurs in the Salisbury and the old Norfolk county records at subsequent dates as follows : 1640, October; 1642, March 5; 1649, February 3 and April 27 ; 1650, December 25 ; 1652, July 18 ; 1657, April 7 and April 14 ; 1662, July 2.

About this time he removed with his family to Ipswich, where we find him Jan. 5, 1663, and again Dec. 22, 1664. He died at Ipswich, May 9, 1665, leaving, says Savage, " a wife Grace and a son *Abraham*.. [† 3.] "

His Will, dated at Ipswich, Jan. 5, 1663, was admitted to Probate, June 26, 1665. An inventory of his estate was returned Sept. 26, 1665, amounting to 230 £. 0 s. 4 d. It has been said that four hundred pounds was about the value of the largest estates in New England in 1661.

His widow was at Ipswich, June 17, and Oct. 9, 1667, and where she died April 25, 1684. She was probably a second wife, since Abraham calls her " mother-in-law." There are some indications that her maiden name was Townsend, since she " appoints her loving brother, Robert Tounsend of Ipswich, her attorney in a suit against Edward Gove." One of the wives of Robert Fitts may have been a Barnes, since his Will mentions " my brother, William Barnes."

Tradition says that previous to his going to Salisbury, Robert Fitts settled in Ipswich, to which plantation he came in 1635 from Fitz-ford,

Tavistock, Devon county, England.   He was a man of education, of high social position, and of Puritan integrity.

> " *Secundo die Septembris*, 1635.

"Theis vnder uritten names are to be transported to St. Christopher's; imbarqued in the William and John,—Rowland Langram, Mr. —— have been examined by the Minister of Grauesend, and tooke the oaths of Alleg. and Suprem : die et A° p'.

> Robert Fitt, 18, [and others]."

Had he been in Virginia still earlier ?

Petition, June, 1628.

"Robert Fitt, Anne his wife, and Alice Harris, a poor widow, to the Privy Council.   Have been 14 years planters in Virginia, and lately brought over 16 hogsheads of tobacco, for which they have not the means to pay custom.   Pray for a warrant for the free discharge of the tobacco, to enable them and their families to return to their planta-tions."

> *State Papers, Colonial Series.*

I. 2.   "RICHARD FITTS and SARA ORDWAY was marryed Octobar 8th, 1654."

He was a kinsman of Robert, and settled first in Ipswich, and after-ward in Newbury.   She is supposed to have been a sister of James Ordway, who was born in Wales about 1620, taxed in Dover in 1649, and about that time moved to Newbury.

"Att the Gen'rall Court holden att New Towne, May 6th, 1635, Wes-sacumcon is allowed by the court to be a plantacon * * * here-after to be called Newberry."   The name of Richard Fitts is in the list of 91 grantees on the Proprietor's Book of Records.   It also is found in town and county records, 1642, Dec. 7 ; 1655, June 30 and Sept. 24 ; 1859, Mar. 25 ; 1661, May 16.

Richard Fitts, called "planter," left no children.   A son, however, of Samuel Symonds, Esq., town clerk, deputy governor, &c., who is supposed by some to have had for his first wife the daughter of Gov. Winthrop, was named after him, Richard Fitts Symonds.

"Richard Fitts dyed Decembar the 24, 1672. * * * Sarah, y⁰ wife of Richard Fitts, dyed April 24, 1667."   His Will, dated Dec. 2, 1672, was presented for Probate, Mar. 25, 1673.   Inventory returned Mar. 25, 1673—164 £. 18 s. 6 d.   He appointed his "well beloved kinsman, Abraham Fitt," executor, and gave him all his lands and his personal estate.

SECOND GENERATION.

II. 1.-3.   "ABRAHAM FFITTS was maried to SARAH TOMSON the (16th) day of May, 1655, by ye worshipfull m'r. Symon Bradstreet.   She was the daughter of Mr. Simon Thompson, who was born about 1610, was in Ipswich 1636, made freeman 1641 or 1648, deeded land to Abraham Fitts 1658, and made his will and died 1676, appointing Abraham Fitts joint executor and heir.

After the death of his first wife, June 5, 1664, Mr. Fitts married the widow of Tyler Birdley, who was in Ipswich 1648.   "ABRAHAM FITT &

REBECCA BIRDLY maryed the 7 of Jan. 1668." She survived him, and in 1679, deeded to her son, Andrew Birdley, all her right in the estate of her first husband, and died June 2, 1709.

Writings having the signature of " Abraham Fitts of Ipswich, Husbandman," bear the following dates: 1667, June 8; 1670, June 6; 1671, May 9; 1672, Feb. 27; 1676, July; 1678, Feb. 18 ; 1680, April 12; 1684. May 17; 1690, Jan. 16.

"Admitted to freedom and took oath accordingly. Abraham ffitt. Ipswich, Mass., Mar. 11, 1673–4."

1675, Nov. 30, with 28 other men from Ipswich, he was impressed for the Narraganset expedition of King Philip's war, in which, on Dec. 19, three Ipswich men were killed and twenty-two wounded. He was also with the expedition to Canada in the year 1690.

He died March 27, 1692. His Will, dated Feb. 24, was presented for Probate, March 29, and the inventory of his estate was returned April 6, all in the year 1692. Appraisement, 366 £. 10 s. ; debts, 98 £. 15 s. 5½ d.

Children of Abraham and Sarah (Thompson) Fitts :
   4. *Sarah*, b. Feb. 21, 1657; d. June 14, 1660.
† 5. *Abraham*, d. 1714.
   6. *Robert*, b. Mar. 30, 1660 ; d. June 15, 1661.
   7. *Sarah*, b. Mar. 15, 1661. Marriage—" William Baker and Sarah Fitts, both of Ipsw., Dece. 30, 1686."

Children of Abraham and Rebecca (Birdley) Fitts :
   8. *Robert*, b. May 28, 1670 ; d. young.
† 9. *Richard*, b. Feb. 26, 1672. (See New Hampshire Branch.)
† 10. *Isaac*, b. July 3, 1675. (See Essex County Branch.).

THIRD GENERATION.

III. 3.–5. ABRAHAM FITTS, JR., of Ipswich, married for his first wife MARGARET CHOAT, the daughter of Sargeant John and Anne Choat, the emigrant ancestors of that distinguished family in the United States. Her father, who was born 1624; and died Dec. 4, 1695, remembered her in his Will, dated 1691, and proved May 1, 1697. " Margaret, wife to Abraham Fitts, died Febr. 28, 1691–2."

Second Marriage :

" ABRAHAM FITTS was married to MARY Ross, Jan^{ur} ye 9th, 1693, [1694]."

Writings between himself and others bear the dates, 1684, May 19 ; 1692, May 27 ; 1693, Dec. 1 ; 1694, April 9 ; 1697 ; 1704, Sept. 11. His Will was dated Aug. 4th, and approved Sept. 13, 1714. Subsequently instruments to and from his widow were given, 1714, Dec. 1, and 1720, July 14. " Augt 16th. The wife of Abr^a Fitts Dep^d this Life, 1739."

Children of Abraham and Margaret (Choat) Fitts :
† 11. *Abraham*, d. June, 1763. (See Bristol County Branch.)
   12. *Ebenezer*, b. Aug. 6, 1685 ; d. young.
   13. *Anna*, b. June 18, 1686 ; d. young.
† 14. *Robert*, b. July 19, 1690. (See Worcester County Branch.)

15. *Anna,* m. Ebenezer Severance of Ipswich.

16. *Margarett,* b. Jan. 25, 1692; m. Ebenezer Grant of Salem.

Children of Abraham and Mary (Ross) Fitts :

17. *Mary,* b. Jan. 8, 1695; d. July 3, 1699.

18. *Mercy,* b. Mar. 3, 1696. "Mercy Fitts (single woman) departed this life y° 25th, Oct°, 1721."

19. *Sarah,* b. Mar. 15, 1698. "Married, annó. 1729, p^r the Rev^d Mr. John Roger, Novemb^r 11, Daniel Wood and Sarah Fitts."

† 20. *Samuel,* b. Aug. 16, 1699. "Samuel Fitts of Ips. & Mary Beadle of York, pub. 3^d day Dec. 1726." He was appointed guardian "unto Ebenezer Fitts, a minor of about seventeen years of age, son of Abraham Fitts, Late of s^d Ipswich, Dec^d, Intestate (?) 27th Mar. 1724." He was afterward a chair-maker in Kittery, Me. (See Maine Branch.)

21. *John,* b. Mar. 31, 1701 ; pub. to Abigail Wood, Feb. 2, 1723. He settled in Ipswich, was appointed guardian to his brother Ephraim, Nov. 26, 1722, and deeded "messuage" to his son Samuel, Apr. 25, 1756. "The wife of Jno. Fitts, shoemaker, died Ap^r 17, 1765." Children : (22), *Abigail,* bap. Feb. 16, 1723 ; d. Feb. 22, 1727. (23), *Mary,* bap. Jan. 14, 1727. (24), *Abigail,* bap. Apr. 6, 1729 ; d. young. (25.) *Samuel,* bap. July 15, 1733 ; m. Hannah Harris, July 6, 1754 ; had a son John bap. by Rev. Nath. Rogers, Feb. 20, 1757, at which time he "own^d y° cov^t ;" signed deeds, 1775, Mar. 2 ; 1785, May 14 ; 1795, Jan. 1, and Mar. 21 ; and d. suddenly Jan. 2, 1796. (26), *Ebenezer,* bap. Feb. 22, and d. Feb. 27, 1736. (27, 28, twins), *Abigail,* d. Feb. 14, 1738 ; *Thomas,* d. July 19, 1739. (29.), *Sarah,* bap. Jan. 19, 1740. (30), *James,* (?) bap. July 12, 1741.

31. *Mary,* b. Mar. 13, 1703 ; m. John Brown, 3^d, of Ipswich.

32. *Ephraim,* bap. Sept. 30, 1705 ; was pub. to Abigail Hodgkins, May 9, 1730. He entered, Apr. 13, 1736, his right on his grandfather's account, and drew, Oct. 27, 1737, Lot. No. 10 in the south division of Ipswich-Canada, now Winchendon, which township was laid out by the General Court, June 10, 1735, "to such as are descendants of the officers and soldiers who served in the expedition to Canada in the year 1690." "Ephraim Fitts died suddenly Jan. 13th, A. Dom^l, 1742."

33. *Ebenezer,* b. Apr. 12, 1708.

New Hampshire Branch.

THIRD GENERATION.

III. 3.–9. "RICHARD FITTS was married to SARAH THORNE, March y⁰ 18th, 169$\frac{4}{5}$."

In 1691, Jan. 16, his father conveyed to him in fee all his lands in Salisbury, which included the original grant to his grandfather, Robert Fitts. He soon afterward moved to Salisbury, where he built a block house for his residence, and to shield his family from the Indians, by whom they were repeatedly attacked. It is a noteworthy circumstance that the same lands are now in possession of his descendants, having never gone out of the family name.

Bonds and conveyances between himself and others, bear the following dates: 1698, Oct. 29; 1700, Feb. 28; 1703, June 2; 1705, Sept. 5; 1709; 1715, Mar. 2; 1717, May 24, and June 14; 1718, Feb. 15, Mar. 9 and July 19; 1739, June 4. His Will was dated July 25, 1741, and admitted to Probate, Jan. 14, 1745. Inventory, Dec. 2, 1745. "Richard Fitts died Dec. 3ᵈ, 1744."

Mrs. Fitts was a superior woman, and remarkable for resolution of character, bravery and piety, walking sixteen miles to worship with the people of God at Ipswich, of which church she was a member. "She was a dutiful and affectionate wife, a kind mother, and a pious, charitable and useful member of society. She died March, 1773, aged 100 years."

Children:

10. *Isaac*, b. Dec. 19, 1695; d. Aug. 10, 1696.

11. *Sarah*, b. July 12, 1697; m. Feb. 8, 1721, Jeremiah Allen, "by y⁰ Reverant Mʳ· Calib Cushing, Pastor of y⁰ Church of Cht., in Salisbury."

† 12. *Nathaniel*, b. July 13, 1699; d. Feb. 6, 1784.

13. *Martha*, b. Feb. 27, 1702; m. Apr. 1, 1727, John Eastman of Salisbury, who was b. Dec. 27, 1701, the great grandson of Roger, the emigrant ancestor of the Eastman family in the United States, having sailed from Southampton, April, 1638, in the Confidence of London, John Jobson, master. Their children were, Jerusha, b. Apr. 21, 1726, m. Samuel Baker, July 27, 1749. Isaac, b. Mar. 30, 1729. John, b. Mar. 20, 1731. Samuel, b. June 28, 1734. James d. in the army at Cape Breton. Richard, b. June 21, 1739. Jacob, b. Apr. 6, 1742, unm.; d. Jan. 1776. Mary, b. Apr. 21, 1744; d. unm. a. 40.

† 14. *Richard*, b. Jan. 20, 1705; d. Feb. 23, 1791.

15. *Ward*, "daugh. borne 9th June, 1707."

† 16. *Daniel*, b. Apr. 30, 1710 ; d. Mar. 30, 1796.

17. *Jerusha*, b. Dec. 10, 1712 ; m. Roger Eastman, a brother of John, Jan. 25, 1730. They settled in Salisbury where their children were : Ezekiel, b. Apr. 28, 1731. Daniel, b. Sep. 29, 1733. Sarah, b. Jan. 10. 1735; m. Wm. Walton, of Salisbury. Abigail, b. Sep. 27, 1730 ; who was the second wife of Col. Ebenezer Webster; m. Oct. 13, 1774 ; d. Apr. 14, 1816 ; and the mother of Mehitabel; of Abigail, who m. Wm. Haddock the father of Hon. Charles Brickett Haddock and William Haddock, Esq., a graduate of D. C. ; of Ezekiel, b. Mar. 11, 1780 ; grad. D. C., 1804 ; and of Hon. Daniel Webster, b. Jan. 18, 1782 ; grad. D. C., 1801 ; d. Oct. 24, 1852.

FOURTH GENERATION.

IV. 9.-12. NATHANIEL FITTS of Salisbury, was published to ABIGAIL HAYES of Dover, N. H., Mar. 18, 1720. "Abigail Fitts, yᵉ wife of Nathaᵈˡ Fitts departed this life June 12, 1738, at 12 o'clock."

Children :

18. *Mary*, b. Feb. 26, 1721 ; m. —— Jackman, and had a son Nathaniel.

19. *Abigail*, b. Jan. 31, 1724.

20. *Rebecca*, b. Dec. 28, 1727. "Eliphalet French and Rebeckah Fitts, both of Salisbury, were married by Caleb Cushing, minister of yᵉ Gospel in Salisbury, April 1, 1747."

Second Marriage :

"NATHANIEL FITTS of Salisbury, entered his intention of marriage with MEHETABLE DERBON of Chester, May 19th, 1744."

Children :

21. *Anna*, b. Mar. 24, 1745 ; m. Daniel Morrill, Jr., May 28, 1763 ; lived in Warren, N. H., and had a son Enoch, who m. Eunice Pearson.

22. *Mehitable*, b. Apr. 26, 1747 ; m. Hophni Flanders, 1766, and d. 1796.

"Mehetabel Fitts, the wife of Dn. Nathᵉˡ Fitts departed this life June yᵉ 11, 1765."

Third Marriage:

DEC. NATHAINEL FITTS and NAOMI MORRILL were published June 6, and married June 18, 1767, by Samuel Webster, Clerk.

"Nahomy Fitt, wife of Dn. Nathaniel Fitts, died Nov. the 21, 1778." Deeds of Nathaniel Fitts, yeoman, bear the dates, 1746 ; 1762, Dec. 7 ; 1765, Feb. 26 ; 1783, Dec. 17. "Dn. Nathaniel Fitts, died Febrʸ the 6, 1784." His Will was dated Apr. 12, 1781, and proved Feb. 22, 1784.

———

IV. 9.-14. RICHARD FITTS of South Hampton, published Mar. 18th, married SARAH BROWN, Apr. 6, 1727. She was born Sept. 14, 1708, daughter of Ephraim and Lydia of Salisbury, a descendant of Henry Brown who came from England and settled in Salisbury about 1640.

Richard Fitts entered into covenant with the Congregational West Church at Salisbury, Mass., Dec. 24, 1727. Sarah Fitts, his wife, united with the same church May 5, 1728. She died about 1754. He afterwards married DOROTHY EVANS of Salisbury, April 1757.

Mr. Fitts settled in what was afterward So. Hampton, N. H., then an uncultivated territory, infested by Indians and requiring in the settlers great energy and fortitude of character. On July 26, 1642, he with 28 others who had "done considerable towards building a meeting house at a place called Logging Plain," gave it to the town which had been incorporated May 27th, preceding. 1754, May 1, he deeded to his son Daniel, fifty acres of land in Kingston. 1756, Mar. 1, he was on a committee appointed by the town to survey a route for a highway. "Mr. Richard Fitts departed this life February the 23, 1791. His Will under date May 3, 1787, was admitted to Probate. Mar. 16, 1791. Inventory returned Apr. 2, 1791.

Children of Sarah :

23. *Sarah*, b. Nov. 27, 1727 ; m. Daniel Quimby of Amesbury, Mass.
† 24. *Daniel*, b. Sep. 25, 1729 ; bap. Oct. 1729.
25. *Nathaniel*, unm. ; d. May 11, 1779.
26. *Elisabeth*, b. Feb. 5, and bap. Mar. 9, 1733 ; pub. to Timothy Flanders of Salisbury, Dec. 2, 1752.
† 27. *Jonathan*, b. July 29, 1734 ; m. Susannah Pike.
28. *Lydia*, b. Nov. 3, bap. Dec. 4, 1737 ; m. Ebenezer Eastman.
29. *Abigail*, b. Sep. 10, 1739 ; m. Nathaniel Morrill of Brentwood.
30. *Mary*, b. May 22, 1743 ; m. Moses Jones of Enfield.
† 31. *Ephraim*, b. May 10, 1745 ; d. Apr. 13, 1800.
32. *Martha*, b. Mar. 13, 1747 ; m. Jonathan King.
33. *Isaac*, b. Mar. 27, 1749 ; unm.; d. Feb. 17, 1778, at Concord, N. H., from disease contracted in the war of the Revolution. Inventory, Mar. 4, 1778.
34. *Anna*, b. Jan. 20, 1751 ; m. Moses Sawyer of Salisbury, N. H., Jan. 16, 1775, and was the mother of Rev. Moses Sawyer, b. Mar. 11, 1776 ; grad. D. C., 1798 ; and of Nathainel Sawyer, Esq., b. Apr. 10, 1784 ; grad. D C., 1805 ; admitted to the bar at Newburyport, Mass., Sept. 1809, and followed the practice of the law at Frankfort, Ky., Chillicothe and Cincinati, Ohio. I am much indebted to valuable manuscripts left by him, in making out this Geneology.
35, 36. Two other children died in infancy.

IV. 9.–16. "DANIEL FITTS and RUTH BROWN were joined in marriage covenant, Pr me Joseph Parsons, Clerk." This was at Salisbury, Mass., Nov. 11, 1734. She was the sister of Sarah who married Richard Fitts the brother of Daniel, and was born 1712, and died June 3, 1788.

Daniel Fitts became celebrated in his trade of a blacksmith for which he served seven years at Ipswich,—" an uncommon good workman, a man of strong, discriminating mind and purpose, great mental energy and decision of character." He conveyed lands by deeds, 1759, Sept. 7 ; 1760, Feb. 23 and Mar. 3. His Will presented for Probate, Apr. 25, 1797, bears date Mar. 4, 1795. Inventory filed June 7, 1796; $1,518.60. "Parson Croffts" of the West Parish attended his funeral.

The following are the inscriptions upon tombstones at East Salisbury :

"In Memory of
MRS. RUTH,
wife of
MR. DANIEL FITZ,
who died
June 3rd, 1788,
in the 73 year of her age.

Life is uncertain, death is sure ;
Sin gives the wound, but Christ yᵉ cure.

In Memory of
MR. DANIEL FITZ,
who died
March 30, 1796,
in the 86th year of his age.

Here darkness dwells
Fit contemplation for human thought."

Children :

† 37.　*Abraham*, b. Oct. 24, 1736 ; d. Aug. 6, 1808.
† 38.　*Nathan*, b. Dec. 13, 1739 ; d. Jan. 29, 1781.
　39.　*Ezekiel*, b. Jan. 15, 1741 ; d. Jan. 16, 1741.
† 40.　*Joseph*, b. Dec. 5, 1741 ; d. Mar. 1, 1823.
　41.　*Ruth*, b. Mar. 3, 1744 ; pub. Nov. 22, and m. Dec. 17, 1777, to Moses Gill, and d. July, 1810, leaving Mary, m. —— Hunt. Daniel d. unm.
　42.　*Mercy*, b. Aug. 6, 1746 ; pub. to Enoch Hoite, Jr., of East Salisbury, Oct. 29, 1768, and d. 1817. He was b. July 17 and bap. July 21. 1745, the son of Enoch of Deerfield, N. H.,—"a stout, resolute, smart man who served under Gen. Stark in the Revolution, and carried his wounded captain, Nathan Sanborn, from the battlefield on his shoulder." Their children were Moses and Hannah, m. —— Morrill.
　43.　*Jerusha*, b. Dec. 7, 1748 ; pub. Dec. 17, 1796, and m. Feb. 3, 1797, to Jeremiah Stevens, and d. Nov. 30, 1818. No children.
　44.　*Abigail*, b. Apr. 5, 1751 ; pub. to Moses Collins of Salisbury, Nov. 4, 1780, and d. Oct. 18, 1826. Their children were Nathan and Enoch, and their descendants occupied the Daniel Fitts homestead in 1868.
　45.　*Elizabeth*, b. Apr. 1753 ; pub. Oct. 8, and m. Nov. 17, 1774, to Enoch Jackman, by Samuel Webster, and d. 1776, a. 23.

FIFTH GENERATION.

V. 14.-24.　DANIEL FITTS married ABIGAIL CURRIER, daughter of Samuel Currier of So. Hampton, and settled in Sandown, N. H., his farm then covered with woods. He gave deeds, 1754, May 1 ; 1758, Nov. 7, and Dec. 8 ; 1759, Mar. 15 ; 1760, Dec. 25 ; 1761, Mar. 20 ; 1781, Jan. 27. His Will was dated at Sandown, July 21, 1783, and presented for Probate, June 15, 1785.

Children, the oldest born in So. Hampton, the others in Sandown.

46. *Hannah*, b. Sept. 21, 1756 ; m. Stephen Hobbs of Poplin, N. H., and had Stephen, Anna, Daniel, Sarah.

† 47. *Richard*, b. Aug. 8, 1758 ; d. Dec. 9, 1826.

48. *Sarah*, b. June 23, 1761 ; m. Noah Scribner of Raymond, and had Anna, Daniel, John, Sylvia, Abigail.

† 49. *Samuel Currier*, b. Aug. 1, 1763 ; d. Jan. 20, 1841.

50. *Betsey*, b. Jan. 26, 1766 ; m. Winthrop Sanborne of Salisbury, N. H., and had John, Elizabeth, m. her cousin Stephen Hobbs ; Ira, Sarah, Daniel, Cyrus, Sargent.

† 51. *Daniel*, b. June 18, 1768 ; d. Jan. 30, 1841.

† 52. *Abel*, b. Mar. 28, 1771 ; d. Mar. 11, 1826.

53. *Nancy*, b. June 29, 1773 ; m. Thomas Quimby of Danville, and had David, Mary, Currier.

54. *Ezekiel*, b. Aug. 5, 1775 ; unm. ; drowned at Vergennes, Vt., May 8, 1826.

55. *Mary*, b. Jan. 29, 1779 ; m. William Bagley of Candia, and' had Currier, Henry, Mary, d. young. She afterward m. —— Baron of Thornton, N. H., by whom she had children.

V. 14.–27. JONATHAN FITTS, married SUSANNAH PIKE of Kensington, N. H., and died 1772, a. 38.

Children :

56. *Sarah*, b. Sept. 30, 1757 ; m. William French.

57. *Mary*, unm.

58 *Elizabeth*, m. Reuben S. Dow.

† 59. *Richard*, ⎫ twins. ⎰ b. Jan. 1767 ; d. Dec. 5, 1836.
60. *Dorothy*, ⎭   ⎱ m. Jan. 21, 1790, Jonathan Currier, by Rev. Nath. Noyes.

61. *Martha*, m. Dec. 18, 1798, Samuel Currier brother of Jonathan, by Rev. Nath. Noyes.

† 62. *Jonathan*, m. Joanna Thurston of Unity, N. H.

V. 14.–31. EPHRAIM FITTS of South Hampton, married RHODA WORTHEN of Chester, N. H., Aug. 29, 1765, by Rev. Mr. Cotton of Sandown. She was born 1743, and died Feb. 28, 1826 ; a. 82.

> " Surviving friends ! her virtues claim
>   A sweet memorial of her name ;
> And while she sleeps in death,
>   It's ours with pious care to tread
> Her steps as far as Jesus led,
>   'Till Heaven demand."

Mr. Fitts learned the trade of a blacksmith with Abraham Fitts (37) in Chester, where he was tithingman 1769, 1772, 1773, besides holding other offices in the town. He was among the soldiers of the Revolution drafted from Chester, and after the war settled in South Hampton. Writings in which he was a party bear date 1778, Feb. 25, Mar. 4, and Apr. 28 ; 1784, May 19 ; 1788, Mar. 9 ; 1792, Dec. 4. He. d. Apr. 13, 1800 ; a. 54. Letters of administration were granted to Rhoda Fitts, widow, and Thomas Worthen Fitts, May 19, and Inventory re-

turned July 4, 1800, $1180.00. Account of administration rendered
Mar. 18, 1807.

Children :
63.   *Sarah*, b. Dec. 13, 1765; m. Thomas Clifford.
64.   *Lydia*, b. Mar. 19, 1768 ; d. Mar. 5, 1778.
† 65.   *Richard*, b. Feb. 22, 1770 ; d. Oct. 6, 1835.
66.   *Elisabeth*, b. Feb. 4, 1772; m. Nathainel Howe of Enfield, N.
H., Feb. 24, 1800, by Rev. Nath. Noyes, and d. 1858 ; a. 86.
† 67.   *Thomas Worthen*, b. Mar. 17, 1774 ; d. June 11, 1813.
68.   *Mary*, b. Sep. 14, 1776 ; m. William Clifford of Candia, May
9, 1823, by Isaiah Palmer, Justice of the Peace.
69.   *Lydia*, b. Feb. 6, 1779; unm.; d. Feb. 7, 1860.
† 70.   *Isaac*, b. Aug. 31, 1781 ; d. Aug. 20, 1854.
† 71.   *Ephraim*, b. June 6, 1784 ; d. Nov. 11, 1842.
† 72.   *Josiah*, b. Sep. 23, 1787 ; d. Oct. 2, 1853.

———

V.* 16.–37. ABRAHAM FITTS of Candia, N. H., married DOROTHY
HALL, May 27, 1760. She was the daughter of Henry Hall of Chester, and died Nov. 8, 1804 ; a. 68.

"Lieut. Abraham Fitts served his time with his father at the blacksmith business. Soon after he became of age, his father put to him as
an apprentice, his brother Nathan, with whom he emigrated to Chester, N. H., then a wild and new town. There he married Dorothy
Hall, and commenced business which he followed four or five years,
and then removed to the adjoining town of Candia. Here he estab-
lished himself in business, and by his industry and frugality, made
himself wealthy, raised a family of ten children, lived highly respected
both in church and state, and died at the age of seventy-two years."

Conveyances of land to and from Abraham Fitts bear the following
dates, 1756, '58, '59, '60, '63, '66, '70, '76, '77, '79, '81, '82, '83, '85,
'89, '90, '91, '93, 1800, 1801, 1803.

He was one of the fourteen original members organized into the
Cong. Church of Candia, 1770. In 1766 he was on a committee to
build a meeting house, and in 1770 bid off pews, 11, 30, 32, and in
1775 purchased Nos. 19 and 21 in the gallery. He was on other committees of the parish, 1766, '68, '69, '70, '71, '79, '80, '81.

Mar. 22, 1763, with 37 others he petitioned for the incorporation of
the town of Candia. July 21, 1774, he was a representative of the
town to choose delegates to the General Congress. In 1776 his name
is on the celebrated Association Test.

"To show our determination in joining our American brothers in de-
fending the lives, liberties and properties of the inhabitants of the
United States :

We, the subscribers, do hereby solemnly engage and promise that
we will to the utmost of our power, at the risque of our lives and for-
tunes, with arms oppose the hostile proceedings of the British fleets
and armies against the United American colonies.

                              Abr'm Fitts [with 98 others]."

In 1777 he volunteered for a short time in the forces of the Revolution, and was at Saratoga when Burgoyne surrendered. The journal
which he kept during the campaign is in the possession of his great

grand son, John Frank Fitts, M. D. In 1780 and again 1782 he was chosen by the town to provide for the families of the soldiers in the war. In 1782 he was appointed to lay before the state the reason why the town object to the proposed plan of government; and in 1784 the first representative of the town to the General Court under the new constitution. He was tithingman of Chester 1762, and of Candia 1773. He was selectman of Chester 1764, and of Candia 1767, '68, '70, '72, '74, '79, '80, 81, '82, '86, '89, '96. He was elected moderator twenty-six times in 1766, '67, '68, '69, '70, '75, '78, '79, '81, '83, '87. Assessor, 1777, '78, '81. Auditor, 1782, '84, '92. On important committees, 1770, '71, '78, '80, '84, '85, '88. School teacher employed by the town, 1776.

It became a common saying in Candia, "Esq. Mooers and Lieut. Fitts rule the town."

He died Aug. 6, 1808; a. 72. His Will dated May 17, was admitted to Probate Aug. 17, 1808.

Children :

73. *Lydia,* b. Mar. 9, 1761 ; m. Moses Emerson of Candia, June 16, 1785, and d. Dec. 17, 1835. Her children were, Moses, June 18, 1766 ; Lydia, July, 12, 1788 ; Susannah, Sep. 26, 1791 ; Jonathan, Dec. 25, 1793 ; John, Feb. 8, 1796 ; Sarah, Mar. 15, 1798 ; Abraham, Sep. 14, 1800, the father of Rev. J. D. Emerson ; Thomas, July 5, 1803 ; Dorothy, May 4, 1806.

64. *Dorothy,* b. Oct. 31, 1762 ; m. Dea. Samuel Cass of Candia, a cousin of the Hon. Lewis Cass. Her children were, Daniel, b. Aug. 8, 1789 ; Samuel, Mar. 17, 1791 ; Moses, Jan. 27, 1793 ; Elizabeth, Jan. 6, 1795 ; Sally, Dec. 28, 1796 ; Mary, Jan. 25, 1799 ; Aaron, Feb. 18, 1801 ; Benjamin, Nov. 13, 1804 ; Dorothy, May 21, 1807. She afterward, 1827, m. Dea. Eben. Nay of Raymond, and d. Mar. 1, 1836.

† 75. *Daniel,* b. Jan. 21, 1765 ; d. Sep. 17, 1829 ; a. 64.

† 76. *Moses,* b. Nov. 14, 1767 ; d Sep. 27, 1838 ; a. 71.

† 77. *Reuben,* b. Mar. 8, 1770 ; d. Sep. 20, 1838 ; a. 68.

78. *Sally,* b. Apr. 20, 1772 ; m. Jonathan Cass of Candia, Oct. 26, 1790, by Rev. Jesse Remington, and d. 1794 ; a. 22. Her children were, Ichabod, Mar. 11, 1791 ; Sally, Nov. 15, 1792.

† 79. *Samuel,* b. July 2, 1774 ; d. June 12, 1850 ; a. 76.

80. *Elisabeth,* b. Apr. 17, 1777 ; became the second wife of Capt. Benaiah Fox, Mar. 13, 1818, and d. Feb. 20, 1823, leaving no children.

† 81. *Abraham,* b. Mar. 22, 1781 ; d. Oct. 31, 1865.

† 82. *Nathan,* b. Feb. 22, 1764 ; d. Dec. 19, 1852 ; a. 68.

———

V. 16.–38. NATHAN FITTS of Chester, married June 8, 1768, ABIGAIL FRENCH, who was born Sep. 4, 1746 ; the second daughter of Major Jabez and Hannah (Hills) French.

Lieut. Nathan Fitts was Auditor, 1770, '76, '79. Selectman, 1776, '77, '78. Committee in 1777, "to allow the soldiers an equality p^r month for the services done in the present war since the commencement thereof."

He died, Jan. 29, 1781 ; a. 43. Letters of administration were granted his widow Feb. 28, 1781. Inventory real estate, 10,395 pounds, personal estate, 20349£. 19s. 4d.

She afterward married Dea. Nath[1] French, and died June 18, 1831 ; a. 84.

Children of Lieut. Nathan and Abigail (French) Fitts :

83.   *Hannah*, b. May 4, 1769 ; m. Moses Sanborn of Sandown, Aug. 11, 1789.

† 84.   *Benjamin*, b. June 6, 1771 ; d. May 20, 1856.

† 85.   *Nathan*, b. Aug. 5, 1774 ; d. Aug. 12, 1825.

86.   *Elizabeth*, b. Apr. 27, 1778 ; m. Daniel Tilton of Sandown.

V.   16.–40.   JOSEPH FITTS of Salisbury, Mass., was twice married. First to MIRIAM MORRILL, Apr. 17, 1770, who was born Feb., 1739, and d. Apr. 12, 1776 ; a. 37. Second to RUHAMAH JUDKINS of Kingston, N. H., who was b. Feb. 28, 1749 ; pub. Nov. 22, 1777, and died Dec. 24, 1840 ; a. 91.

Mr. Fitts settled as a blacksmith and farmer on the homestead in Salisbury, of which town he was for nine years a Selectman. He deeded lands in 1777, '81, '83, '87, '90, '95, 1807, '10. For the last dozen years of his life he was confined to his bed by paralysis. During all this time he was a great reader, and a cheerful and pious man. He died Mar. 1, 1823 ; a. 83. His Will dated Nov. 17, 1809, was presented for Probate "the last Tuesday in March, 1823." It named his widow and son Moses joint executors, but she declined the trust and Moses was appointed sole executor, Mar. 24, 1823. Inventory filed "the last Tuesday in June, 1823." Amount, $2037.76.

Children of Joseph and Miriam :

87.   *Mary*, b. June 20, 1772 ; pub. Aug. 15, and m. Nov. 30, 1801, to John French of Salisbury, and had one son Benjamim.

† 88.   *Isaiah*, b. Apr. 5, 1776.

Children of Joseph and Ruhamah :

89.   *Miriam*, b. Jan. 3, 1779 ; pub. Oct. 31, and m. Nov. 26, 1807, to Samuel Morrill of Amesbury. No children.

90.   *Elisabeth*, b. Feb. 23, 1780 ; pub. July 7, and m. Aug. 1, 1804, to Jeremiah Sawyer of Salisbury. Her children were Enoch, Moses, Joseph, Eliza, Sarah, Jeremiah.

91.   *Lucy*, b. Feb. 20, 1782; pub. Mar. 21, and m. May 12, 1806, to William Ordway of Amesbury, and had Ruhamah, Lucy, Ann, Hannah, French.

92.   *Lois*, b. June 25, 1784 ; unm. ; d. Apr. 8, 1842. Her Will was signed Apr. 2, 1842, and presented for Probate, June 14, 1842.

93.   *Eunice*, b. Sep. 20, 1787 ; pub. Apr. 16, and m. June 16, 1808, to John Griffin, and had Joanne and a child died in infancy.

† 94.   *Moses*, b. May 31 ; bap. July 3, 1791.

SIXTH   GENERATION.

VI.   24.–47.   RICHARD FITTS married DOROTHA KIMBALL of Freemont, and settled in Sandown. On Feb. 2, 1795, he entered a protest of himself and seventeen others on the town records, against certain proceedings connected with the settlement of Rev. John Webber. In 1796, Oct. 28, he deeded land in Sandown to Daniel Fitts of Boston. He died Dec. 9, 1826 ; a. 68.

"A tender husband, father dear,
A much lamented friend lies here ;
When Christ returns to call him forth,
The rising day will show his worth."

Tombstone.

Letters of administration on his estate were granted to Cyrus Fitts, Jan. 11, 1827. Inventory, $1264.97. His widow died Jan. 4, 1848 ; a. 80. Power of administration was granted to Nathainel Fitts, Aug. 1, 1848.

"And art thou gone my mother dear !
And has thy spirit fled
And left its earthly dwelling here
To mingle with the dead !"

Tombstone.

Their children were .

† 95. *Daniel*, b. Mar. 7, 1789; settled in Salisbury, N.H., and afterward in Boscawen, where he died July 13, 1865. He was twice married, first to Abigail Mitchell of Sandown, Nov. 12, 1812, second to Sarah Ann Weeks of Hopkinton, Mar. 17, 1846. Children all by his first wife : Almira, Mary B., Harriet E., m. John Colby, George W., twice married, and lived in Cambridgeport, Mass., and Lawrence, Kansas, John Mitchell, M. D., m. —— Chase, an eminent physician in Warner and South Sutton, N. H., Cyrus, m. Elisabeth Courser, and settled in Webster, Orlando H., Daniel. Two others d. in infancy.

† 96. *Richard*, b. Dec. 6, 1790 ; m. first, Mary, the daughter of Hon. Joseph Blanchard of Chester, by whom he had Maria Blanchard, m. Garland Califf; Sally, m. Israel Tibbetts ; Mary Ann, m. Abbott Danforth He m. second, Maria Stevens, and had Rhoda Jane, who m. Alpheus Bullard. He d. in Boscawen, N. H., Jan. 10, 1846.

97. *Nancy*, b. Mar. 2, 1792 ; m. John Tibbetts and lived in Charlestown, Mass. No children.

† 98. *Abel*, b. Oct. 26, 1793 ; m. April, 1820, Sally Locke of Lexington, Mass., who was b. May 26, 1792 ; d. Aug. 2. 1865, and had Sarah Ann, Feb. 1, 1821, m. Daniel Pratt ; Mary Jane, Sept. 28, 1822, m. Nathan Tufts ; Charlotte Temple, June 10, 1824, m. Gilbert Tufts ; Harriet Elisabeth, July 11, 1828, m. Charles Augustus Jenks ; Nathan Everett, Feb. 24, 1830, m. Harriet A. Magoon ; George Hammond, May 24, 1833, m. Rebecca S. Moulton.

Abel Fitz, Esq., was an able business man, residing in Lexington, and afterward in Summerville, Mass., where he was assessor of the town for several years, and acquired in the grain business an estate exceeding in value, $100,000. He died May 23, 1856, and was buried in Mt. Auburn cemetery.

99. *Mary*, b. May 29, 1797 ; m. Nathaniel Abbot of Boscawen, N. II., Dec. 3, 1827. He was b. Aug. 11, 1796, the son of Josaph, a pensioner of the Revolution, having served in Col. Peabody's regiment. . Children : Horace, Nov. 23, 1829 ; Mary Jane, June 5, 1831 ; d. Oct. 1, 1834 ; Maria F., Mar. 28, 1833 ; Julia Ann, May 22, 1834 ; Mary Jane, 2^d, Jan. 7, 1836 ; George Whitefield, Mar. 13, 1837.

100. *Cyrus*, b. Aug. 24, 1798 ; unm. Appointed guardian to his sister Cynthia, Mar. 3, 1827. Died Dec. 24, 1845. Will dated June 14, 1844. Inventory, Feb. 12, 1846.

" O may this death remind us all,
That here we've no abiding place;
But the next shaft of death that falls,
May call us to our resting place."

Tombstone.

† 101. *Nathaniel*, b. Sep. 28, 1800 ; m. Rhoda Purington who was b. Apr. 6, 1801, and d. Nov. 20, 1848. They settled in Sandown where he d. Mar. 14, 1867. Children: Richard, Mar. 29, 1827, d. unm., Sep. 25, 1863 ; Rhoda Jane, Feb. 20, 1829, m. David Sanborne of Freemont, and d. Nov. 4, 1863 ; Charlotte, Jan. 28, 1832, m. Henry A. Mayo of Milo, Me. ; Abel, Mar. 5, 1834, m. Emily Susan Fuller, May 1, 1861, and had Charles Abel and Charles ; Franklin, Feb. 26, 1836, m. Nov. 26, 1857, Abbie Sawyer, and had Addie May ; Sarah Ann, Sep. 29, 1840, m. Wm. E. Clough, Aug. 1, 1858, and d. June 29, 1859.

102. *Sally*, b. June 28, 1802.

† 103. *Hiram*, b. Oct. 30, 1807 ; m. Mary Jane Currier of Hampstead, July 28, 1842. She was b. Sep. 18, 1816, the dau. of John and Hannah, and d. Mar. 12, 1854. He settled opposite the Cong. meeting house in Sandown. Children: Marion, July 20, 1844, d. Sep. 14, 1644 ; Infant son, July 27, 1845, d. same day; Hellen Kimball, Sep. 20, 1846 ; Edwin Cyrus, Apr. 16, 1849 ; Frances Marion, Jan. 1650, d. young ; Twins, Mary Jane and Martha, Sep. 15, 1852, the latter dying in infancy.

104. *Cynthia*, b. Nov. 11, 1809. She was the second wife of David Lane of Chester, and had children : Franklin, Harriet, Mary, Josephine, Lauren, Samuel.

———

VI. 24.–49. CURRIER FITZ married SARAH GEORGE of Hampstead, and settled first in Sandown, and then in Derry, N. H. Mr. Fitz was remarkable for physical strength and mental energy, and became quite wealthy. He either gave or received deeds of land in 1788, '96, '97, 1806, '07, '09, '14, '15. He died Jan. 20, 1841 ; a. 77 ; leaving his widow who died June 10, 1846 ; a. 81.

Their children were:

105. *Sarah*, b. Nov. 5, 1793 ; m. Col. Samuel Adams of Derry, and had Caroline, Louisa, and George.

† 106. *Daniel*, b. May 28. 1795 ; m. Sep. 5, 1826, Caroline Fitz Sawyer, dau. of Rev. Moses and Fanny (Kimball) Sawyer of Salisbury, N. H., by whom he had children all born in Ipswich, Mass ,—Sarah Adams, June 30, 1827, d. Nov. 21, 1848, m. Joseph Barbien Walker, grad. Yale, 1844, attorney and counsellor at law, Concord, N. H. ; George Currier, Apr. 14, 1830, m. Mary B. Crofut, Feb. 9, 1854, and had George Lendrum and Daniel ; Louisa Adams, May 17, 1833, d. Oct. 17, 1847 ; Twins, Daniel Francis and Caroline Frances, Aug. 14, 1837. The former, Daniel Francis, grad. H. U., 1859, attorney and counsellor in Boston, m. Oct. 10, 1865, Mary Frances, dau. of Wm. F. and Mary P. Wade of Summerville. The latter, Caroline Frances, m. Sep. 1, 1858, Joseph W. Woods, a merchant in Boston.

Rev. Daniel Fitz, D. D., grad. D. C., 1818, and at Andover Theological Seminary, 1825. He was ordained colleague pastor with Rev. Joseph Dana, D. D., of Ipswich, Mass., in 1826, and remained in the pastoral office until 1867, when he resigned its active duties. He has published several discourses. His first wife d. Jan. 10, 1862 ; a. 57, and he m. Mrs. Hannah Bardwell Demond of Westboro', Mass., Apr. 14, 1863.

107. *George*, b. June 23, 1800 ; grad, D. C. 1822, and became Rector of Mt. Zion College, South Carolina, dying at Winnsboro', in that State, Mar. 29, 1826. "A talented and promising young man."

VI. 24.–51. Daniel Fitts married Hannah French. "February 27th, 1798. The within persons were married about half after 4 o'clock even. By me John Webber."

She was born May 25, 1780, the daughter of Esq. Ebenezer and Rhoda (Barnard) French of South Hampton. They settled in Sandown, where he gave deeds in 1798, 1800 and 1801; was town clerk, 1800, and auditor, 1806. In 1808, with thirteen others he petitioned the town for a proportionate division of the parsonage money and the use of the meeting house among the different denominations; and the town "Voted to grant the request of Daniel Fitts and others by a petition in regard to the parsonage." Mr. Fitts died, intestate, Jan. 30, 1841; a. 73. Hannah, his widow, was appointed administratrix May 12, and returned inventory Aug. 11, 1841.

Their children were :

108. *Frances*, b. Aug. 31, 1798 ; m. John Sanborne of Chester, June 1821, the son of Jethro and Hannah (Foss) Sanborne, and had Sarah Maria and Olive Frances.

109. *Rhoda*, b. Jan. 16, 1800 ; m. Dec. 2, 1819. Josiah Hoyt of Sandown, Justice of the Peace and Quorum, Member of the Legislature, &c. Only one son, Daniel R.

† 110. *Ebenezer*, b. Jan. 31, 1802 ; m. Louisa Brown, Nov. 1824, and settled in Sandown, where she d. May 25, 1843 ; a. 39, and he survived till Aug. 13, 1854. Their children were : Abel Brown, Apr. 10, 1825 ; d. Oct. 31, 1828. Ruth Emily, Feb. 4, 1827 ; m. her cousin Dr. John Sanborne, son of Betsey (111). Martha Elisabeth, Sep. 22, 1829 ; d. Oct. 16, 1848.

111. *Betsey*, b. July 6, 1804 ; m. Nov. 1824, Rufus Sanborne, the brother of John, and had Dr. John ; Luther C., a wealthy grain merchant at Sioux city, Iowa ; Josiah R. ; Mary Elisabeth ; and twins, J. Frank and Frances M.

112. *Sarah*, b. Jan. 10, 1807 ; m. James Brown of Auburn, June 1839, and had Elisabeth Langford, d. young ; Daniel Barnard, d. in infancy ; Willis Harlan, d. six days after returning from the army, Aug. 14, 1863, a. 19 ; Abel ; Woodbury.

113. *Hannah Byenton*, b. June 19, 1814 ; m. her cousin, Lyman Fitts (119,) of Vershire, Vt., June 12, 1838.

VI. 24.–52. Abel Fitz of Vershire, Vt., married Betsey George of Sandown, N. H., Jan. 10, 1801. She was born Mar. 24, 1779, and died May 4, 1857, the daughter of Joshua and Anna (Currier) George of South Hampton. He bought land in Sandown, 1797 ; sold land and a "Pew in Sandown Meeting House, No. 2," to Danial Fitts, in 1798 ;

was tithingman in 1800 ; afterward moved to Vermont and died Mar.
11, 1826.

Their children were:

114. *Nancy,* b. Jan. 1, 1802 ; m. Dec. 31, 1829, Jonathan B.
Jewell, who was b. May 24, 1803, and d. Aug. 10, 1852, and had
children, George A. F., June 13, 1831 ; d Oct. 26, 1833. Maria S.,
Aug. 20, 1832 ; m. Eli Jewett, Apr. 15, 1855. George F, June 15,
1835 ; m. Susan Sargent, Oct. 23, 1855. Caroline E., Apr. 9, 1838 ;
m. Albion Wyman, Dec. 27, 1855. Orwell, Dec. 4, 1844.

† 115. *Currier,* b. Aug. 15, 1803 ; m. first, Mar. 25, 1833, Jemima
E. George, who d. Feb. 10, 1850, and had Cynthia D., Jan. 9, 1834 ;
d. Sep. 30, 1844. Carrie Sleeper, Sep. 17, 1835. J. George, June 8,
1837 ; m. Victoria Avery, June 16, 1863. Abel, Aug. 4, 1839. Nancy
S., Oct. 4, 1841. John W. M., Jan. 11, 1845. Mary Ann, Dec. 26,
1849 ; d. May 11, 1850. He m. second, Sophia Cheney, Apr. 18,
1851, who d. Aug. 22, 1863 ; by whom he had Charlie A., Mar. 8,
1852 ; d. Sep. 6, 1853. Mary E., Dec. 7, 1853. Cora L., May 24,
1856.

116. *Sally,* b. June 20, 1805 ; m. Israel Mattoon, Nov. 20, 1828,
and had John L., Dec. 1830. Orwell, 1833.

† 117. *Daniel,* b. Jan. 3, 1808 ; m. Elmira Sawyer, Aug. 2, 1838,
who d. Sep. 11, 1864, and had children : Mary J., Aug. 23, 1840 ; m.
Giles R. Durkee, Mar. 2. 1862. Julia A., May 15, 1842 ; m. Charles
W. Heath, Apr. 30, 1865. Lucina, July 14, 1845. James M., Mar.
5, 1847. Emeline, Oct. 26, 1850. Hiram, May 20, 1857. Homer,
Aug. 19, 1859.

118. *George,* b.·Oct. 2, 1811 ; d. Feb. 17, 1821.

† 119. *Lyman,* b. June 21, 1815 ; m. his cousin, Hannah Byenton Fitz
(113), June 12, 1838 ; settled in Vershire and had Elisabeth A., May
12. 1839 ; m. Henry Bryant, Oct. 9, 1865. Ellen Augusta, Sep. 18,
1842. Samuel Houston, Apr. 26, 1851. Frank Richard, Dec. 21,
1852. Daniel Webster, Jan. 6, 1855.

———

VI. 27.–59. Richard Fitts married Elisabeth Currier, Mar. 28,
1792, by Rev. Nath. Noyes, and settled in South Hampton, where he
died Dec. 5, 1836, and she survived till July 20, 1847 ; a. 80. His
Will dated Nov. 21, 1836, was presented for Probate, Jan. 11, 1837.
Inventory, Apr. 12, 1837.

Their children were:

120. *Joseph,* b. Aug. 5, 1792 ; unm. He lived at Newton, N. H.,
and d. intestate, Nov. 8, 1848. Thomas J. Goodwin, administrator,
Jan. 10, 1849.

121. *Polly,* b. Mar. 1795 ; unm.

† 122. *Chellis,* b. Feb. 17, 1796 ; m. Hannah R. Peaslee of Newton,
Feb. 28, 1828, and moved to Dumbarton, N. H., where she d. July 28,
1865 ; a. 65. Their children were, Hannah Elisabeth, Nov. 10, 1829 ;
d. Jan. 17, 1835. Caroline Louisa, Sep. 23, 1831 ; d. Jan. 14, 1835.
Harriet Alvira, May 29, 1833. Richard Peaslee, July 12, 1837.
Lewis Challis, May 23, 1842 ; m. Esther Ann Goodwin of Concord,
Apr. 5, 1866.·

123. *Elisabeth*, b. 1798 ; m. Richard Peaslee of Newton, and had Hiram, Aug. 4, 1831, m. Mary Ann Carlton ; and Richard, m. Catherine Mehitable Thompson, who was b. Nov. 3, 1834.

124. *Richard*, b. June, 1800 ; m. Abigail Stevens, who d. Apr. 7, 1853 ; a. 36   He lived in South Hampton, where his only son, John W., d. May 10, 1852 ; a. 8 mos.

† 125. *William*, b. 1802 ; m. Elisabeth Abbott of Newburyport, lived in Kensington, N. H., and d. Aug. 29, 1844.   Children : Mary Elisabeth, d. May 23, 1843 ; a. 17.   William Francis ; Joanne ; Benjamin.

126. *Jonathan*, m. Abigail Dow, and lived in Kensington.   No children.

127. *Sally*, m. Rufus Dow, settled in So. Hampton, and had Rufus Franklin.

128. *Nathaniel*, unm. ; lived in So. Hampton.

129. *Almira*, m. Anson Gile of South Hampton, Apr. 30, 1834, and had, Sarah ; Ellen ; Mary Ann ; Lorena ; Frank.

VI.   27.–62.   JONATHAN FITTS married JOANNA THURSTON of Unity, N. H.   He settled in Unity, but afterward moved to Smithfield, N. Y., and again about 1814 to the State of Michigan.

Their children were :

130. *Jonathan*, lived in Ohio and had eleven children.

131. *Anna.*

132. *Elisabeth*, whose second husband was Silas Betts of Oxford, N. Y.

133. *Sally.*

134. *Lavinia*, m. John Carpenter of McDonnough, N. Y.

135. *Hiram*, lived in McDonnough.

VI.   31.–65.   RICHARD FITTS married Aug. 1796, MARY POWELL, who was born at Henniker, N. H., Dec. 13, 1776.   He first lived in Dorchester, N .H., where he was one of the early settlers, about 1791, afterward in Enfield, 1804, then moved to East Hanover on the celebrated "cold Friday," Jan. 19, 1810, driving his ox-team ten or twelve miles in a farmer's frock with no overcoat.   He died Oct. 6, 1835.

Their children were :

136. *Joanna*, b. Sep. 22, 1798 ; m. Mar. 1824, Francis Withington, who was b. Apr. 11, 1796, and d. Sep. 27, 1864.   Children : Oscar R., Mar. 29, 1826 ; Moses E., Jan. 31, 1828 ; Ephraim F., Jan. 21, 1830 ; Richard W., a twin, Oct. 27, 1832 ; Rhoda Ann, also b. Oct. 27, 1832 ; Lorinda C., Oct. 21, 1836 ; Convers F., July 24, 1839.

137. *Lydia*, b. Sep. 29, 1800 ; m. Apr. 10, 1823, Wm. M. Withington, b. Apr. 8. 1801, and had Gardner F., Jan. 25, 1824 ; Sylvester, Apr. 12, 1825 ; Elias, Dec. 4, 1829 ; R. M., Jan. 25, 1831 ; Mary N., June 8, 1833 ; Pluma, July 7, 1837 ; William G., Jan. 25, 1841.

138. *Rhoda*, b. Sep. 28, 1802 ; m. Feb. 16, 1825, Isaac D. Stark, and had Alfred D., May 23, 1827 ; Isaac G., June 16, 1829 ; Alonzo, Dec. 18, 1834 ; Mary Ann, June 29, 1838 ; Ireneus, Jan. 25, 1841.

139. *Ephraim*, b. July 22, 1805 ; d. Sep. 3. 1806.

† 140. *Convers*, b. Oct. 6, 1808 ; m. Lydia Bryant, Mar. 7, 1839, and

3

settled on the homestead in Hanover, N. H. Children: Henry T., Jan. 27, 1840 ; m. Emma Marden, June 21, 1864. Rhoda Rosette, Aug. 12, 1848.

† 141. *Richard,* b. Oct. 19, 1813 ; m. Mary D. Rogers, Nov. 28, 1849, and lived in Hanover. The children were : Lorenzo R., Aug. 20, 1852 ; d. Aug. 19, 1858. Alvin W., and Irving P., twins, July 26, 1856.

† 142. *Dexter,* b. Dec. 13, 1818 ; m. Sarah Hill, June 6, 1853, and lived in Concord, N. H., and had Eva, Apr. 1856.

———

VI. 31.–67. THOMAS WORTHEN FITTS married SARAH FRENCH of South Hampton, Nov. 28, 1799, by Rev. Nathainel Noyes. They settled in Dorchester, N. H., where he died, June 11, 1813 ; a. 39. She died Mar. 7, 1866 ; a. 85.

Their children were :

143. *Parmelia,* b. July 17, 1801 ; m. Elihu Woodman of Kingston, and had Elisabeth ; Sarah.

† 144. *Thomas Jefferson,* b. Dec. 21, 1802 ; m. Thankful F. Moore of Dorchester, Dec. 29, 1829. He was a highly esteemed citizen of Dorchester, Justice of the Peace, and member of the Legislature, 1848 and 1849. Children, all born in Dorchester: Emily C., Sep. 14, 1830 ; Sarah, May 27, 1832 ; d. May 25, 1834. Sarah E., Apr. 26, 1834 ; m. Darius Capron. Elisabeth K., June 4, 1836. Mary A., Apr. 20, 1838 ; m. Isaac Davis. Charles H., Nov. 14, 1840 ; d. May 20, 1852. John M., Apr. 25, 1843.

† 145. *Daniel French,* b. Apr. 2, 1805 ; m. Susan Fellows of Danville, N. H. He settled in Haverhill, Mass., as a boot and shoe manufacturer, held many city offices and was representative to the General Court in 1847. Children: Laura Ann, Dec. 5, 1826 ; m. Albert H. West ; d. Nov. 18, 1866, and had George and Charles, both d. young ; and Mary, b. Apr. 1858. Daniel, Feb. 14, 1830 ; m. Sarah W. Appleton, Nov. 1, 1853, and had Sarah Alice ; Helen Louise ; Edward Appleton ; Annie Hazen ; Charles Frederick. Charles Hazen, Jan. 30, 1833. Stephen Warren, Mar. 15, 1835 ; m. Mary A. Chick, and had Susan Matthews ; James Warren. Susan Emily, June 18, 1837. Henry Thomas, Jan. 30, 1842, 22d Reg. Mass. Vols.

146. *Sarah,* b. Jan. 14, 1807 ; m. Russell F. Clifford of Warren, 1829, and had Ruth ; Thomas J. ; William ; Sarah ; Russell S. ; Zachariah.

147. *Drusilla,* b. Jan. 28, 1809 ; d. Feb. 8, 1809.

† 148. *Joseph,* b. Dec. 28, 1810 ; m. Hannah Rowell, Oct. 8, 1834, who was b. Aug. 12, 1813, and settled as a shoe manufacturer at Haverhill, Mass. Children : Alfred Metcalf, Dec. 12, 1836 ; drowned in the Merrimack, June 30, 1858. Mary Frances, Jan. 17, 1839. Warren Jacob, June 7, 1841 ; commissioned 2nd Lieutenant 35th Reg., Jan. 14, 1865. Leroy Benson, Oct. 5, 1846. Hannah Philena, Apr. 13, 1849 ; d. July 29, 1850. Horace Lucian, Jan. 10, 1852.

149. *Elisabeth,* b. Dec. 24, 1812 ; m. Joseph Magoon of East Kingston, and had Sophronia ; Samuel Allen ; Calvin ; Caroline ; George ; Mary.

VI. 31.–70. " Isaac Fitts of South Hampton, entered his intention of marriage with Nancy Bagly of Salisbury, July 30, 1814." They were married, Sept. 25th, and settled in Dorchester, N. H., where he died, Aug. 20, 1854; a. 74.

Their children were:

150. *Lucien*, b. Aug. 23, 1815.
151. *Anna*, b. May 5, 1817; d. May 11. 1836.
152. *George W.*, b. Jan. 3, 1819; d. Oct. 2, 1859. His Will dated at Franklin, N. H., Sept. 26, 1859, mentioned his wife, Clara A., and his "only and infant son," and was presented for Probate the fourth Tuesday of October, 1859.
153. *Charlotte T.*, b Feb. 26, 1822 ; m. John B. Richardson of Candia, at Lowell, Nov. 4, 1846, and settled as a boot and shoe manu-facturer in Haverhill, Mass.
154. *Drusilla*, b. Dec. 29, 1823.
155. *Ephraim*, b. Oct. 14, 1826; m. and settled in Rumney, N. H.
156. *James Gilman*, b. Nov. 30, 1829.

VI. 31.–71. Ephraim Fitts of South Hampton, married Rachel Goodwin, Nov. 29, 1800. She died Dec. 30, 1863; a. 83 yrs., 4 mos., 5 days.

> " With her the toils of life are o'er ;—
> She has gone to the realms of the blest,
> To dwell with Christ for evermore,
> And there enjoy the promised rest."

Mr. Fitts represented the town of South Hampton in the Legislature two years, and was Selectman in 1811, '12, '13, '16, '20, '24, '25. He died Nov. 11, 1842 ; a. 58.

> " When death has severed earthly ties,
> The loss must cause a sigh ;
> But with unshaken faith in Christ,
> We know 'tis gain to die.
>
> Surviving friends ! mourn not for me,
> But bow beneath the rod,
> And let your highest effort be,
> Prepare to meet thy God."

Their children were :
157. *Maria*, b. Jan. 11, 1808 ; m.
158. *Rebecca*, b. June 30, 1810 ; m. Ebenezer Peaslee, Feb. 1832.
† 159. *George W.*, b. May 29, 1812; m. Ruth B. Ingalls, May 22, 1844, by Rev. Abiah Kidder. She was b. Apr. 5, 1813 ; dau. of Israel and Mary (Currier) Ingalls. They lived in South Hampton, Concord, and Exeter, N. H. He represented the town of South Hampton in the Legislature in 1845, and was Selectman in 1838, '42, '43, '46, '63. Their children were : Mary Josephine, Feb. 19, 1845 ; Ruth Annie, Sep. 15, 1846 ; Frances Place, May 9, 1849 ; George Ephraim, Dec. 29, 1851 ; d. Dec. 11, 1855. Judith Bell Currier, Mar. 6, 1855.

160. *Mary Ann,* b. Oct. 29, 1818; m. Almon Drake, and d. Apr. 11, 1858.

VI. 31.–72. Josiah Fitts married Susannah Gale of Amesbury, 1811. She was the daughter of Capt. E. Gale of the Revolution, and born Jan. 23, 1791. They lived in South Hampton and Candia, N. H., where he died, Nov. 1, 1853. His Will dated May 20, 1852, was admitted to Probate, Nov. 9, 1853. Inventory, Jan. 11, 1854.

Children, all born in South Hampton:

161. *Sarah Ann,* b. Aug. 31, 1812; m Sargent Currier of Amesbury, Mass., Nov. 24, 1831, and had Eliza Jane, Dec. 3, 1833, and Monroe S., May 19, 1840.

† 162. *Andrew Jackson,* b. Apr. 14, 1815. He changed his name for Harrison; m. Ann Pilsbury of South Hampton, Sep. 13, 1846, and had Ann Louisa, Apr. 26, 1848; Florence M., June 25, 1851.

163. *Susannah,* b. June 18, 1817; m. Josiah Clifford, Esq., of Candia, May 11, 1837, and had Thomas H., Apr. 15, 1842.

† 164 *Josiah Monroe,* b. Aug. 2. 1821; m. Mary Cass, and settled in Candia, where he had Mary C., Mar. 25, 1844; m. Leonard F. Dearborn, Feb. 12, 1862. Monroe Gale, May 7, 1847; d. Sep. 20, 1848.

† 165. *Stephen Burt,* b. Dec. 17, 1823; m. Mary Josephine Richardson, June 30, 1844. He was a Justice of the Peace at Candia, N. H.; Auditor in 1849; Selectman, 1850; Constable, Collector and Juror, 1852; Moderator, 1853; and died at Rye, Aug. 31, 1860. The children were: Roselette Jane, May 4, 1849; d. Dec. 28, 1863. Willie Burt, June 5, 1855.

† 166. *James Gale,* b. May 31, 1827; m. Martha Ann Pilsbury of South Hampton, and settled in Newton, N. J., as hotel-keeper. He was captain in the War of the Rebellion, and served on Gen. Carney's staff.

He had children,—three daughters.

VI. 37.–75. Daniel Fitts of Candia, N. H., married Rachel French of Salisbury, Mass., Mar. 3, 1790. She was born, Sep. 29, 1762, and died at Candia, June 21, 1830.

Mr. Fitts was a Justice of the Peace, and a capable man in business. His deeds of real estate bear the dates, 1789, 1800, '01, '02, '04, '05, '16. He was Tithingman, 1799, 1818; Assessor, 1799; Auditor, 1802, '06, '09, '10, '19, '21; Selectman, 1803, '07, '08, '13, '14, '15, '16, '17; Moderator, 1806, '07, '08, '10, '14, '15, '17, '18; Committee of Parish, 1812, '18; School Committee, 1815, '17, '18, '20; Special Town Committee, 1818, '23, '26; Juror, 1828; Overseer of the Poor, 1826, and "directed to use all lawful means to stop the progress of intemperance, or any other vicious habit which in their opinion may have a tendency to increase the number of paupers."

Daniel Fitts, Esq., died Sep. 17, 1829. His Will dated, Feb. 2, with a codicil, May 13, was admitted to Probate, Oct. 14, 1829.

Children were:

167. *Mary,* b. Dec. 9, 1790; unm.; d. Sep. 5, 1818.

168. *Salome,* b. Nov. 11, 1792; m. Moses Bursiel, Jr., and d. May

17, 1830, leaving Rufus, Jan. 29, 1815 ; Salome French, Mar. 16, 1816, a deaf mute ; Mary Fitts, Mar. 3, 1819 ; Francis, m.

† 169. *Daniel,* b Dec. 4, 1894 ; m. first, Nancy Hall of Bradford, Mass., by whom he had George, Nov. 10, 1820 ; bap. Feb. 25, 1821 ; d. unm., May 15, 1851 ; a portrait painter. Elisabeth Hall, bap. Aug 27, 1826 ; d. Mar. 31, 1827. Elisabeth Ann Hall, bap. 1830 ; d. Mar. 1, 1834. He m. second, Mrs. Lucinda (Johnson) Kimball of Bradford, Mass., Dec. 12, 1854. She was b. Oct. 25, 1806, the dau. of Dea. Thomas and Lydia (Noyes) Johnson of East Haverhill, Mass. He was baptized and admitted to the Cong. church in Candia, Nov. 17, 1822, of which he was chosen Deacon about 1824. He ·was widely known as a succsssful teacher, and was on the school committee of Candia for seven years. He was elected Auditor, 1820, '27 ; Juror, 1820, '21, '26 ; Selectman, 1826 ; Committee of Church, 1824, '25, '29, '30, '31, '32, '33, '35 ; Church treasurer for four years, 1827, and again in 1833 ; Clerk of church, 1832 ; and of the Cong. Society from its organization, May 1831. About 1836, Dea. Fitts moved to Bradford, Mass., where he was Town Clerk some ten years, and clerk of the Cong. church to the time of his death, April, 1861.

† 170. *Joseph,* b. Oct. 13, 1796 ; m. Mahala Buswell of Candia. She was b. Dec. 14, 1799, the dau. of John and grand daughter of Samuel Buswell, who enlished in the French War and was at Cape Breton, and also in the Revolutionary War with Gen. Stark. Capt. Joseph Fitts was bap. Jan. 12, 1823, and with his wife united with the Cong. church in Candia, but was suspended, Dec. 25, 1825. He held the office of Sexton for many years, and d. April, 1862. Their children were : Harriet, May 12, 1822 ; m. Samuel S. Johnson of Northwood, Sep. 13, 1842. Mary, June 22, 1823 ; m. Luther Flint of Candia, Feb. 5, 1845. Mahala, July 5, 1825 ; m. George R. Bean of Candia, Feb. 19, 1846, and d. Apr. 27, 1846. Elisabeth, Aug. 9, 1828 ; m. John Pillsbury Bean, Sep. 18, 1855, and settled in the West. Emily Jane, Apr. 19, 1840 ; m. Joseph W. Randall of Deerfield, June 4, 1857. Catherine Brown, July 1, 1832 ; d. June 11, 1849. Mehitable Ann, July 4, 1834 ; m. Capt. W. M. Quimby of Raymond, Nov. 29, 1854, and d. at Portland, Me , Jan. 9, 1857 ; Nancy Maria, Dec. 25, 1836 ; m. June 2, 1861, Wells C. Haynes, who d. July 21, 1861, of wounds received at the battle of Bull Run. John Frank, Aug. 24, 1839 ; attended medical lectures at Hanover, N. H., and at New York city, where he received his diploma, 1866, and settled as a physician at Francistown, N. H.

171. *Rachel,* b. Mar. 9, 1799 ; m. John Pillsbury of Candia, 1821, and d. Nov. 8, 1822.

172. *Benjamin,* b. Aug. 1, 1801 ; d. May 4, 1823.

173. *Judith Hall,* b. Sep. 24, 1803 ; united with the Cong. church, 1823 ; d. unm., Nov. 6, 1833. Her Will dated, Aug. 22, and approved, Nov. 13, 1833, beside remembering many relations, bequeated a legacy to the New Hampshire Missionary Society.

† 174. *Abraham,* b. Aug. 28, 1805 ; m. Mary Emerson of Raymond, June 20, 1827. Capt. Abraham Fitts and his wife united with the Cong. church at Candia, May 6, 1838, where he d. May 3, 1840. Their children were : Isaac, Apr. 12, 1828 ; bap. May 27, 1838. Martha, Oct. 2, 1831 ; d. Oct. 12, 1831. Mary, Nov. 19, 1832 ; bap. May

27, 1838 ; m. Edmund E. Smith of Candia, June 17, 1857.   Abraham, d. in infancy, Sep. 20, 1837.

VI. 37.–76. MOSES FITTS of Candia, married SARAH ORDWAY, Apr. 19, 1797. She was the grand daughter of Rev. Nehemiah Ordway, D. D., of Amesbury, Mass., and born July 8, 1774, and died July 31, 1823.

"Master Fitts," disabled by rheumatic difficulties in early life, entered upon the profession of teaching, and upon mercantile pursuits. Tradition says he owned the first chaise in town ; and his infirmity was regarded as sufficient excuse for indulging in such a luxury. Deeds of real estate passed between himself and others : 1790, '92, '95, '99, 1800, '06, '07, '08, '09, '11, '12. He was chosen Auditor, 1793, '94, 1805, '15 ; Licensed Innholder, 1798, '99, 1815 ; Moderator, 1799, 1803 ; Selectman, 1802 ; Representative to General Court, 1809, '10 ; Tithingman, 1815 ; Committee of Parish, 1818 ; Sealer of weights and measures, 1821 to 1824, inclusive. He united with the Cong. church in Candia, 1832, and died Sep. 27, 1838. His Will dated, Apr. 28, was recorded, Oct. 10, 1838.

Children were :

175. *Sophia*, b. Aug. 17, 1798 ; d. Dec. 1, 1814 ; a. 16.

176. *Sally*, b. Mar. 26, 1800 ; united with the Cong. church, 1823 ; m. Dr. Nathaniel Wheat of Candia, President of the New Hampshire Musical Society, &c., and was the mother of Thomas Wheat, M. D., grad. Jefferson Medical College, Philadelphia, and practiced at Manchester, N. H. She d. Oct. 8, 1866.

† 177. *Frederick*, b. June 21, 1802 ; m. Lucinda French of Candia, Oct. 21, 1824. She was b. June 18, 1803, and united with the Cong. church in 1823. He was Postmaster of Candia for many years ; Licensed Innholder in 1824, '27, '28 ; Town Clerk, 1831 ; Collector of Taxes, 1837 ; and in a season of deep mental depression, drowned himself, Nov. 3, 1837. The children were : Martha Ann, Nov. 24, 1825 ; bap. Sep. 1, 1826 ; united with Cong. church in 1843, and d. Oct. 7, 1845. Infant daughter, d. Nov. 14, 1826. Infant son, d. Sep. 18, 1827. Alfred Dana, Aug. 30, 1829 ; united with Cong. church, 1849 ; m. Olive Jane, dau. of Emery and Mary (Hubbard) Currier of Candia, and d. Jan. 12, 1864, leaving George Dana, b. Feb. 28, 1860. Twins, Apr. 27, 1832, one d. May 15, and the other, May 24, 1832. Sarah Jane, Mar. 31, 1835 ; united with Cong. church in 1855 ; m. John S. Patten of Candia, Dec. 21, 1857, and had Ella Florence. Charles Frederick, July 27, 1837 ; united with the Cong. church in 1856 ; m. Oct. 3, 1867, Anna Maria, dau. of Frederick and Hannah (Dutton) Seavy.

† 178. *Moses Hall*, b. Jan. 1, 1808 ; m. Rachel J. Harrison, who was born in the city of Buffalo, N. Y., Oct. 6, 1816. He graduated at D.C., 1831, and became a teacher and member of the Board of Education for the State of New York, " Worthily distinguished in the cause of education, he has not wanted flattering testimonials of his merit at the hands of the people and government." His children were : A child, d. in infancy, Apr. 8, 1836. Sarah Elizabeth, Nov. 3, 1837, Principal of Riverside Seminary, Saginaw City, Mich.   James Franklin, Sep.

11, 1839; admitted to practice of the law at Buffalo, in 1860; was Major under Gen. Banks in the War of the Rebellion, an army correspondent during the War, and a contributor the "Galaxy" afterward, entering the firm of Holmes and Fitts, attorneys, &c., Lockport, N. Y. Willard Cooke, Dec. 24, 1842; entered the U. S. service where he lost health of body and mind through the attrocities of Libby Prison. Mary Harrison, July. 5, 1845; teacher in Palmyra Classical School, N. Y. Edward Henry, July 5, 1848. Charlotte, Coleman, Feb. 2, 1851. Florence, Jan. 25, 1854.

† 179. *Franklin*, b. June 23, 1811; m. Emily, dau. of Capt. Jesse and Sarah (Prince) Eaton of Candia. He attended medical lectures at Hanover, N. H., commenced practice at Buffalo, N. Y., in 1835, and soon after died.

180. *Alfred*, b. Sep. 1, 1814; d. Sep. 17, 1841.

VI. 37.–77. "MR. REUBEN FITTS and MISS ANNE HILL, both of Candia, were married, November 14th, 1792." This was by Rev. Jesse Remmington, pastor of the Cong. church in Candia. She was born, Feb. 28, 1769, the daughter of Jethro and Mehitable (Jewett) Hill, who came from Stratham to Candia in 1765. Mr Fitts and his wife united with the Cong. church in Candia some time previous to 1816. He was on a committee of the parish to supply the pulpit in 1818, and a committee of the church for disciplice in 1823, '32, '34. He died intestate, Sept. 20, 1838; a. 68.

Children were:

† 181. *John*, b. Mar. 19, 1794; m. Abigail, who was born, Dec. 22, 1798, the eleventh and youngest child of Esq. John and Hannah (Godfrey) Lane, and the sister of Susannan Lane, who m. Abraham Fitts (81). John Fitts connected himself with the Cong. church in Candia in 1823, and Abigail Lone, afterward his wife, the same year. He was chosed Tithingman, 1823, '31; Assessor of Society, 1822, '49, and of Town, 1829; Juror, 1831; Collector of Society, 1834, '37; Committee of Church, 1834, '35, '43, '45, '53, '56, '63. Their children were: James Hill, Mar. 3, 1829; bap. Sep. 1829; graduated at Bangor Theological Seminary, 1858; ordained as an evangelist, Nov. 2, 1859; installed at West Boylston, Mass., Sep. 3, 1862; m. Mary Celina, dau. of Dea. Coffin M., and Dolly (Pilsbury) French of Candia, Jan. 1, 1862. Hannah Lane, Mar. 1, 1831; united with the Cong. church in Candia, Mar. 1849; a teacher at the North, and among the Freedmen South. John Lane, Dec. 8, 1834; m. Augusta J. Smith of Candia; served in the Army from 1851 to 1864, a good portion of the time in the rebel prisons of Richmond, Salisbury and New Orleans. After the War he settled in Candia near the homestead where he was selectman of the town for several years; in 1865 held a justice commission, and was a surveyor and licensed conveyancer of land.

† 182 *Joshua*, b. Dec. 3, 1799; m. Sarah Knowles, Apr. 27, 1826, by Rev. Abraham Wheeler. They settled in Candia, where he united with the Cong. church in 1823, and his wife with the same church in 1843. Their children were: Amos Knowles, June 26, 1827; bap. Dec. 1827; united with the Cong. church in 1843, and d. Mar 19, 1850. Reuben Hill, July 7, 1829; m. Almira J. Fife of Deerfield, N.

H., June 18, 1857, who d. Nov. 4, 1865, leaving Mary Abbie, Feb. 26, 1863. He volunteered and joined the U. S. forces in the War of the Rebellion, Co. K. 1st N. H. Heavy Artillery, Sep. 21, 1864. William Garland, Nov. 9, 1833 ; m. Martha Ann Brown of Candia ; pub. June 30, 1855, united with the Cong. church, July 5, 1857 ; volunteered in the Army of the U. S. during the Rebellion ; and had children : Sarah Elisabeth, Mar. 27, 1859, and Willie Amos, May 22, 1861. Elias, b. Nov. 5, 1837 ; d. Jan. 25, 1841. Eliza Ann, Feb. 19, 1839 ; united with Cong. church, 1857.

183. *Eliza*, b. Dec. 12, 1802 ; united with the Cong. church at Candia, 1832, and d. unm., Sep. 14, 1838.

184. *Phebe*, b. Apr. 5, 1805 ; m. John Carter, and settled in Lancaster, N. H. Their children : Lauraette, July 4, 1840 ; d. 1846. Reuben Fitts, May 1, 1842. Nancy Hill, June 11, 1845 ; d. Oct. 9, 1864. Phebe Fitts, May 12, 1847. Arlette, June 12, 1849. Peter, Oct. 15, 1850.

VI. 37.–79. " MR. SAM⁰ˡ FITTS and MRS. SARAH TOWLE, both of Candia, were married, December 15ᵗʰ, 1796." She was born, Feb. 7, 1777, and died, Oct. 23, 1831.

Mr. Fitts was elected Tithingman of Candia in 1809 and 1826, and Assessor, 1829. He was a man eminent for piety, and with his wife united with the Cong. church previous to 1823, when under the partoral care of Rev. Abraham Wheeler. He was committee of church for discipline, 1825, '33, '45 ; committee for church visitation, 1829, '35 ; standing committee, 1829, '35 ; and died June 12, 1850.

Their children were :

185. *Lydia*, b. Aug. 25, 1798 ; united with Cong. church, 1823 ; m. Joshua Lane of Candia, Sep. 11, 1821.

186. *Sarah*, b. Sep. 25, 1801 ; bap. Apr. 16, 1820, united with Cong. church, 1832 ; m Jonathan Brown of Candia, Mar. 6, 1822, and had seven sons : Alfred m. and settled in Dracut, Mass. John Newton, m. Nov. 30, 1854, Elizabeth Minerva, dau. of Joel and Clara (Metcalf) Hunt of Medway, and had issue, Elizabeth Agnes, Nov. 16, 1859, ob. Sept. 5, 1860 ; Charles Nathan, Jan. 6, 1861 ; Caroline Maria, Jan. 7, 1864. Jonathan C., grad. D. C, 1854. Benjamin Franklin, m. Sarah Dalrymple, and had Frank ; Fred ; George. Samuel Newell, d. young. George Boardman. Charles Henry.

187. *Clarissa*, b. June 23, 1804 ; bap. Apr. 16, 1820, united with the Cong. church, 1823 ; m. John Emerson of Candia, Feb. 2, 1823, and d. May 30, 1865. He was the grandson of Col. Nathaniel Emerson who served as an officer under George III, and also in the War of the Revolution under Gen. Stark, and afterward eight or ten years in the N. H. Militia,—nor was he less distinguished in civil than in military stations. The children of Clarissa (Fitts) Emerson were : Richard ; Sarah Jane ; Sophronia ; Henry Martyn ; Lydia ; Ann Judson ; John Sherburn ; George Champion, d. in the Union Army, 1861 ; Abbie Lane ; Frederick Fitts ; Horace Mann.

† 188. . *Asa*, b. Nov. 16, 1810 ; bap Apr 26, 1820 ; m. Susan Burroughs, who was b. Apr. 1803, and d. July, 1855. They resided at Candia and Kingston, N. H., and Roxbury and Boston, Mass.

Mr. Fitz was a successful teacher of music in the Teachers' Institutes of Mass., and a well-known author and publisher of music, school and philosophical works. Their children were : Charles Frederick, d. in infancy, June 24, 1834. Charles Frederick and Ellen Eliza, b. Mar. 1835 ; bap. July 2, 1835. Susan. Charles Frederick was a clerk of Suffolk and of Old Boston banks ; m. June 19, 1863, Annie Gibson Cummings, b. in Boston, Jan. 6, 1842, the dau. of Daniel Gibson and Maria Louisa Cummings, and had issue: Abby Manly, b. in Roxbury, Jan. 3, 1866.

VI. 37.–81. '' MR. ABRAHAM FITTS, JU^r., and MISS SUSANNAH LANE, both of Candia, were married, May 30th, 1804.''
She was born, Ap. 22, 1777, the daughter of Esq. John and Hannah (Godfrey) Lane, and died, May 29, 1865 ; a. 87. Among her brothers were Joshua, who married Lydia Fitts, (185.) Joseph, the father of Rev. Charles W. Lane, Professor in Oglethorpe University, Georgia. Esq. John, whose daughter Emily married Hon. Frederick Smyth, Governor of N. H. Dr. Isaiah, the father of Rev. James P. Lane of Andover, Mass.
During the war of 1812, Capt Lang and Lieut. Hubbard having declined to perform the duty, Ensign Abraham Fitts proceeded to draft the quota of soldiers for the town of Candia. He was chosen assessor, 1808 ; auditor, 1822 ; grand juror, 1836 ; and culler of staves and surveyor of lumber for 15 years. He became connected with the Cong. society at its organization, May 1831, of which he was moderator, 1833 ; auditor, 1834 ; and committee to procure a parsonage, 1837. In 1838 he and his wife united with the Cong. church—she being baptized, May 6th—and he was appointed committee of church for discipline, 1846. He died Tuesday, Oct. 31, 1865.
Their children were :
189. *Dorothy*, b. Feb. 18, 1805 ; d. Apr. 24, 1807.
† 190. *John Lane*, b. July 24, 1806 ; m. Louisa Woodman, June 10, 1832. They lived in Lowell where he was Deacon of the First Cong. church, two or three years a member of the city council, and in 1841 and 1843, represented the city in the Legislature ; then in Candia, N. H., where he was invited to retain his official relations to the church, of which he was auditor and clerk ; afterward in Epping and Freemont, N. H. Their children were : Daniel Brainard, Nov. 30, 1836 ; grad. Poughkeepsie Business College, 1865. John Milton, July 23, 1838 ; m. Angeline Fredrika Tuck of Freemont, Jan. 2, 1860. Louisa Isabella, Apr. 5, 1841 ; d. Aug. 14, 1844. Abraham, Feb. 1, 1847. Infant son, d. Jan. 13, 1850.
† 191. *Isaac Newton*, b. Nov. 15, 1808 ; settled in Lowell as a machinist, and was for one or two years a member of the city council. He m. first, Eliza Ann Peabody of New Bedford, N. H., who was b. Mar. 28, 1811, and d. Oct. 17, 1842, and had issue : Newton, Sep. 30, 1833 ; m. Climena Williams of North Anson, Me., Sep. 5, 1853, and had Ann Stewart, Oct. 15, 1854 ; d. July 1867—an organist and civil engineer in Norfolk, Va., and other cities of the Union. Mary Jane, Apr. 14, 1836 ; m. David L. Hill, Sep. 8, 1855, and d. at Lowell, July 19, 1856, leaving Minnie Fitts, June 12, 1856. Mr. Fitts m. for his

4

second wife, Harriet N. Peabody, Feb. 16, 1843—a sister to his first wife. Children: Clarence Frank, May 7, 1846; d. 1847. Frank Eugene, May 26, 1848; a clerk in Boston. Adelaid Eliza, June 9, 1853; d. Mar. 20, 1854. Wilfred Lincoln, June 13, 1856.

192. *Dorothy*, b. Apr. 17, 1810; united by letter from Lowell with the Cong. church in Candia, June, 1837; m. Joshua Dean of Manchester, N. H., and d. Aug. 25, 1849.

193. *Hannah Godfrey*, b. Nov. 22, 1811; united with the Cong. church in Candia by letter from the Third Cong. church in Lowell, June, 1837; m Alonzo Chadwick of Boscawen, N. H., and d. Nov. 24, 1854, leaving Fitz Henry; m. —— Wheaton, Nov. 1867, and George.

194. *Sabrina*. b. May 11, 1813; m. Dec. 31, 1835, Dea. Hayden Higley of Epping and Raymond, N. H., who was b. at Canton, Ct., Sep. 13, 1810. Children: Elma Ann, Jan. 27, 1837; m. Chas. A. Shepard, Oct. 23, 1866. Harlan Page, June 27, 1839; m. Ann Rollins, 1860, and d. in the Union Army at Carrolton, La., Nov. 24, 1862.

† 195. *Jesse Remmington,* b. Mar. 5, 1815; m. Caroline Phelps of Groton, N. H., May, 1841. He settled in Candia where he was selectman, 1848, '49; auditor, 1852; juror, 1857; auditor of Cong. society, 1843, '52, '54, '58, '59, '62, '63; committee of church or society, 1844, '53, '55, '56, '58, '65; assessor of society, 1845, '46, '64, '65; moderator of society, 1851, '60, '63; superintendent of Sabbath school, 1864, 1865. Their children were: Carlos Eustace, b. Jan. 20; bap. Sep. 1, 1843; d. June 28, 1861. Nathan Corydon, b. June 14; bap. Dec. 11, 1844; grad. National Business College, Poughkeepsie, N. Y., 1865. Emmagene, b. June 9, and bap. Nov. 2, 1849. Alice Caroline, b. Sep. 24, 1852; bap. Sep. 27, 1854.

† 196. *Abraham*, b. Aug. 26, 1817; m. first, Emily, the dau. of Nathainel Morrell of Canterbury, N. H., June 7, 1843, who d. Oct, 23, 1845; a. 24; leaving Charles Abbion, July 29, 1845; member of the Union church, Worcester, Mass., Nov. 1863; enlisted in the 57th Reg. Mass. Vol.; wounded at the battle of the Wilderness, and d. at Armory Square Hospital, Washington, D. C., June 17, 1864. He m. second, Mary Ingalls, dau. of Dea. Josiah and Abigail (Shaw) Chase of Chester, N. H., Jan. 28, 1846, and had Mary Emma, Dec. 16, 1848. William Henry, Aug. 1, 1855; d. Nov. 26, 1855. Mr. Fitts was a machinist at East Boston, Manchester, N. H., and Worcester, Mass., and was the patentee of Fitts' Boiler Feeder, and Globe Gates, &c.

197. *Ruth Lane*, b. Mar. 16, 1819; united with the Cong. church, 1838; was eminent in christian virtue, and d. unm., Feb. 19, 1846.

† 198. *Benaiah*, b. Apr. 14, 1821; a machinist and inventor at Worcester, Mass.; m. Abby A. Manahan, Oct. 21, 1851, of New London, N. H. Children born in Worcester were: Carrie Evelyn, July 3, 1854. Homer, Nov. 19, 1856. Ellen Montgomery, Jan. 7, 1859. Edson, Oct. 28, 1863; d. Oct. 5, 1864.

199. *Susan*, b. Jan. 3, 1824; m. Joshua Dean, Mar. 19, 1850, and was a successful singer and teacher of vocal and instrumental music.

———

VI. 37.–82. "Mr. NATHAN FITTS and MISS NANCY DEARBORN, both of Candia, were married, July 10th, 1805." She was the daughter of

Edward Dearborn, Esq., and Susannah, his wife, of Deerfield, N. H., and was descended "from the same stock of Gen. Henry Dearborn of known repute." Mr. Fitts first settled on a farm in Candia, but afterward moved several times. Before leaving Candia he was chosen tithingman in 1811 and 1815; auditor, 1817; moderator, 1819. He was b. the same day with his wife, Feb. 20, 1784, and d. Dec. 19, 1852. She d. Aug. 1862.

Their children were:

† 200. *Christopher Columbus*, b. Sep. 5, 1806; m. Lois De. Merritt of Hampton, N. H., Nov. 1827; settled in Wisconsin, was killed by falling from a building, Oct. 28, 1854, and had Sarah T., John D., Davis D.

† 201. *Edward Dearborn*, b. Mar. 6. 1808; m. 1836, Eliza Ann Dodge of Grantham, N. H., and had: Francis, Nathan D., Edna. With his wife he joined the Shakers at Canterbury, N. H., was afterward divorced, and in 1866, m. Adaline Spinney.

202. *Mary*, b. July 11, 1811; m. Aaron Town, Mar. 1833, and had ten children.

203. *Isaac Jones*, b. Mar. 24, 1816; d. Apr. 5, 1817.

† 204. *Isaac*, b. May 12, 1818; m. Ann M. Shackford of Pembroke, N. H., Apr. 1, 1841, and lived in Bedford and Manchester, N. H. Children: Charles H., Feb. 16, 1842; a corporal 12th Reg. Mass. Vol. Hellen A. June 22, 1843; m. Joseph R. Weston, Jan. 10, 1865. Frank W., July 16, 1846; a clerk at Manchester. Adda S., Jan. 20, 1849.

205. *Sarah*, b. Sep. 24, 1825; m. Albert Corliss, Mar. 16, 1851, and had: Josephine, Nathan, Mary, Lenora, John E., Walter A.

VI. 38.–84. BENJAMIN FITZ of Chester, N. H., married first, HANNAH HOYT, who was born, June 17, 1776, and died, Oct. 11, 1797; a. 21.

> "I've pass'd the solemn hour of death;
> My friends and relatives I've left;
> O may they be prepared to die,
> To live and reign with Christ on high."

He married for his second wife, SUSANNAH DEARBORN, Apr. 10, 1798, who was born, June 22, 1775, the daughter of Dea. John S., and Mary (Emerson) Dearborn of Chester. Capt. Benjamin Fitz settled as a blacksmith on the homestead in Chester, where he was chosen constable in 1806; auditor, 1812, 1824; and selectman, 1816. With his wife he united with the Cong. church, 1823; and died, May 20, 1856; a. 86. She fell into the fire at the old mansion, and died, Apr. 15, 1860; a. 84 yrs. 10 mos.

The children of Benjamin and Hannah (Hoyt) Fitz were:

206. *Sarah*, b. Jan. 27, 1791; m. Moses Robie, who was b. Apr. 15, 1787, and had issue: Rufus, July 29, 1811; m. Emeline Brown, June 28, 1835. Cyrus, July 13, 1813; m. Sarah Judkins, May 21, 1836. Moses Collins, July 19, 1816. Sarah F., June 18, 1818; m. Josiah Flanders. Caroline F., Aug. 16, 1821; m. Augustus Lernec. Hannah E., Oct. 16, 1830; m. George E. Hersey, July 19, 1854.

207. *Elisabeth,* b. Feb. 3, 1796 ; m. Matthew Holmes of Londonderry, N. H. ; selectman in 1848, 1849. He was descended from the celebrated Scotch Irish stock, the grandson of John who came to this country with his father Abraham in 1719. Issue, one son who has been town clerk, &c., and four daughters. She d. Feb. 2, 1856.

Children of Benjamin and Susannah (Dearborn) Fitz :

208. *Susan,* b. Feb. 28, 1799 ; m. John Tabor, Dec. 1822, and lived in Dracut, Mass. Issue : Ann Mary, May 4, 1824 ; m. Orford Blood. Charles, Aug. 5, 1826. Susan Jane, Aug. 5, 1828 ; m. Horatio N. Marshall. Caroline, Feb· 26, 1831. Ben. Franklin, Aug. 5, 1833. John Frank, Dec. 1836 ; m. Laura Coburn. Sarah Emeline, Dec. 26, 1838. Caroline Bell, Feb. 15, 1843. "All singers, and I never saw a Fitts that could not sing."

† 209. *Benjamin,* b. Mar. 21, 1800 ; m. Oct. 29, 1835, by Rev. Jonathan Clement, D. D., Climena Green, who was born, July 15, 1814, the dau. of True and Sally H. (Collins) Green of Deerfield, N. H. Benjamin Fitz united with the Cong. church in Chester, Nov. 11, 1819, of which he was elected Deacon as early as 1842, and clerk, Nov. 9, 1843. He was selectman of Chester in 1832, '33, '40, '42, '43 ; juror, 1841 ; treasurer, 1842 ; auditor, 1843 ; town clerk, 1844. He d. Aug. 5, 1851. Children : Luther Francis, Oct. 17, 1842 ; d. Sep. 17, 1858. Charles Edwin, Jan. 23, 1845. Ann Louisa, Aug. 7, 1846 ; d. Apr. 22, 1848. Arthur Green, Aug. 10, 1848. Alice Jenniss, Mar. 6, 1851. Emily Sarah Green, Mar. 22, 1853. Parker Green, bap. Jan. 1, 1850 ; d. young.

† 210. *Nathan,* b. Mar. 3, 1803 ; lived at Chester, N. H., and Springfield, Mass. ; m. first, Judith Colby, Oct. 30, 1826. She was b. in Lynn, Mass., July 4, 1803, and d. at Springfield, Mass., Feb. 25, 1846. Children : Mary Ann, Nov. 22, 1827. Warren Colburn, Jan. 23, 1830. John Dearborn, Dec. 28, 1832 ; m. Fanny Peck of the "Bell Ringers." James Ames, Oct. 23, 1833 ; d. Oct. 21, 1834. Caroline Frances, July 10, 1835 ; d. Aug. 17, 1848. George Washington, May 18, 1837 ; d. Feb. 17, 1848. Adeline Celesta, July 19, 1838. Luther, Nov. 10, 1839 ; d. Jan. 29, 1840. Ellen Maria, Sep. 18, 1841 ; d. July 29, 1842. Charles Morton, Nov. 13, 1842 ; d. Mar. 23, 1857. Frank Leroy, Jan. 17, 1844 ; d. July 11, 1844. Nathan Fitz, m. second, Martha Russell, Oct. 10, 1850, and had Frank Russell, Nov. 7, 1851 ; d. Jan. 23, 1863. Lydia Lizebeth, Sep. 2, 1853 ; d. Jan. 27, 1863.

† 211. *Charles,* b. Sep. 13, 1805 ; d. July 11, 1832 ; m. first, Hannah Bartlett of Newbury, Mass., and had Charles Norton, 1832 ; and m. second, Rebecca Morse, and had George Calvin, m. Stevens.

212. *Mary,* b. Feb. 2, 1809 ; united with the Cong. church in Chester, July 15, 1832 ; m. Frederick Morse of Manchester, N. H., and had Henry F., and Rosetta.

213. *John Dearborn,* b. Apr. 11, 1811 ; d. Dec. 12, 1831.

† 214. *George Washington,* b. Aug. 16, 1813 ; united with the Cong. church in Chester, Mar. 18, 1832 ; m. May 3, 1841, Catherine Van Horn, who was b. in Springfield, Mass., Apr. 19, 1814, and settled in Chicopee, Mass., where he had issue : Edward Southworth, Sep. 6, 1842, a teacher connected with the Freedman's Bureau, and grad. of A. C. Arthur L., Feb. 8, 1847.

215. *Hannah H.,* b. July 28, 1816 ; united with the Cong. church,

Dec. 11, 1831 ; m. first, Joseph Chase, and had Algenon, who d. of sunstroke in the Army ; and a daughter ; m. second, John Langley, and had three daughters.

† 216. *Luther*, b. Jan. 13, 1819 ; m. Elisabeth F. Haseltine, who was b. Dec. 10, 1817, and settled on the homestead in Chester, as a farmer and produce dealer. Their children were : Elisabeth H., Mar. 4, 1846. Helen Louisa, Dec. 19, 1848 ; d. Aug. 3, 1850. Ella Louisa, Feb. 1, 1852. Mary Adelaide, Aug. 10, 1854. Henrietta Caroline, May 18, 1856 ; d. Mar. 4, 1857. Sarah Josephine, Mar. 23, 1858. Isabel Henrietta, Jan. 20, 1863.

217. *Ann Caroline*, b. May 1, 1821 ; d. Mar. 10, 1822.

VI. 38.–85. NATHAN FITZ married HANNAH MORSE and settled in Chester, though he seems to have lived in Sandown for a time. In 1793 he was a subscriber for Hopkins' System of Divinity, 2 vols. ; received deeds, 1797, 1805 ; gave deed of land, 1797 ; was chosen constable, 1817, and died, Aug. 12, 1825 ; a. 5ł. His Will dated, Aug. 2, 1825, was presented for Probate, Oct. 30, 1825, and the Executor's account allowed, Aug. 16, 1827. Inventory, $3917.59. No children.

VI. 40.–88. ISAIAH FITTS of Salisbury, Mass., and HANNAH HOOK were published, Nov. 8, and married, Nov. 27, 1800. He settled near the homestead, and had large possessions in upland, meadow and marsh, and died, May 12, 1843 ; a. 67. His Will dated, Apr. 10, 1843, was presented for Probate, June 13, 1843. Inventory, $7854.33. Account of administration on the estate of his widow was returned, Mar. 4, 1845.

Their children were :

218. *Miriam Morrill*, b. Sep. 12, 1801 ; m. John Pike, Jr., and had Isaiah Fitts, and Hannah.

219. *Anna*, b. Jan. 17, 1804 ; m. Jabez True, son of Rev. Jabez True of Salisbury. Issue : Caroline, m. Azor O. Webster, for many years town clerk, &c., of Salisbury. Oliver ; Albert ; Ida ; Lillie, who became the second wife of A. O. Webster, Esq.

† 220. *William Hook*, b. Oct. 29, 1806 ; pub. to Hannah Locke of Seabrook, N. H., Aug. 3, 1833 ; settled in Salisbury and had Mary Locke, Jan. 1, 1835 ; d. Jan. 11, 1854.

221. *John*, b. Aug. 18, 1820 ; d. Feb. 6, 1842.

VI. 40.–94. MOSES FITTS of Salisbury, married first, SARAH TILTON of Kensington, N. H. ; published, Aug. 26, and married, Nov. 24, 1815, who died, May 17, 1817 ; a. 26. Second, LOIS EASTMAN of Kensington ; published, Oct. 28, 1820, who died, Sep. 17, 1822 ; a. 30. Third, LOUISA BOYINGTON of Dedham, Mass. ; published, Oct. 2, 1824, who died, Nov. 22, 1832 ; a. 39, and fourth, MARIAH FRENCH ; published, Nov. 23, 1833, who died of a cancer, Apr. 17, 1862.

Mr. Fitts settled as a farmer on the homestead in Salisbury, which had descended by inheritance in the family from its first settlement in

1639; and he was the last surviving member of his generation in this branch of the family, though for many years nearly disabled by rheumatism.

Children of Moses and Sarah (Tilton) Fitts:

222.   *Sarah Tilton*, b. Feb. 28, 1817; m. Abraham Collins of Salisbury; pub. Aug. 6, 1842, and had Ellen Maria; Anna K.

Children of Moses and Lois (Eastman) Fitts:

† 222.   *Joseph*, b. June 23, 1822; pub. to Mary E. Hilton of Kensington, N. H., Dec. 6, 1847; settled in Salisbury, and had John Prescott, Nov. 13, 1848.

Children of Moses and Louisa (Boynton) Fitts:

224.   *Almeria Euphratia*, b. Oct. 28, 1826; d. Feb. 12, 1850.

225.   *Abigail Ruhamah*, b. Sep. 10, 1831; d. Oct. 4, 1851.

Children of Moses and Maria (French) Fitts:

226.   *Louisa M.*, b. Jan. 17, 1835; united with the church, Nov. 30, 1851; m. Moses N. Bartlett of Salisbury, and had Maria, Mar. 17, 1867.

227.   *Elisabeth Augusta*, b. July 20, 1849; d. Dec. 24, 1851.

> "Dear little one! thy pains are ended,
> Thou hast found a better land;
> Thy songs are now with angels blended
> Where no death or sorrow come."

Essex County Branch.

THIRD GENERATION.

III. 3.–10. ISAAC FITTS of Ipswich, married first, BETHIA ———— and lived in Salem and Ipswich. She died, Aug. 23, 1722. His second wife was the widow MARY NOYES; published, Apr. 20, and married, June 5, 1723, by Rev. Moses Hale. She was born, May 1, 1682, the eldest daughter of Thomas and Judith (March) Thorley of Newbury. Her father was the son of Richard of Rowley; born, 1632; married, 1670, and died, July 11, 1689. A deed of uplands and marsh in Newbury was given by "Isaac Fitts of Ipswich, Glover," May 9, 1746. He died, Apr. 6, 1747.

Children of Isaac and Bethia Fitts:

† 11. *Isaac*, bap. Apr. 17, 1698.
12. *Rebecca*, bap. May 29, 1700.
13. *Bethia*, bap. Oct. 4, 1702.
† 14. *John*, twice married.
15. *Sarah*, b. Oct. 12, 1705.
† 16. *Jeremiah*, b. Jan. 9, 1708; d. Feb. 3, 1801.
17. *Ruth*, b. May 6, 1711.
18. *Abigail*, b. Apr. 12, 1713; d. young.
19. *George*, b. Apr. 15, 1716; d. in infancy,
† 20. *James*, b. June 1, 1718.
21. *Abraham*, b. Aug. 9, 1719.
22. *George*, bap. July 23, 1721; d. Aug. 22, 1721.

Children of Isaac and Mary (Noyes) Fitts:

23. *Abigail*, bab. Sep. 8, 1728.

FOURTH GENERATION.

IV. 10.–11. "ISAAC FITTS, JUNR. and ABIGAIL SHERWIN, both of Ipswich, were published the thirty-first day of March, 1722." She was the daughter of John and his second wife, Mary (Chandler) Sherwin, and born, May, 1695, and died, Jan. 18, 1745. After the death of his first wife, Isaac Fitts married RUTH JONES of Topsfield; published, Jan. 18, 1746. He was a hatter, and died intestate in Danvers, owning land and a barn in Topsfield, and his widow, Ruth Fitts, was appointed administratrix, Sep. 3, 1753. Sixteen years after, Dec. 26, 1769, she, still a widow in Danvers, gave a deed to Mehitabel Babson.

Children of Isaac and Abigail (Sherwin) Fitts : *(*
24. *James*, bap.,Sep. 21, 1723.
25. *Mary*, bap. July 10, 1726.
26. *Abigail*, d. Dec. 18, 1729.
27. *Isaac*, bap. Mar. 15, 1729 ; d. July 8, 1731.
28. *Lucy*, bap. Jan. 3, 1730 ; m. Joseph Smith.
29. *Abigail*, bap. Oct. 3, 1731, "admitted into full communion with the First Church in Ipswich, Nov. 15th, 1761 ; * * * * died suddenly at Deacon Lord's, March 12th, 1796."
30. *Isaac*, bap. Sep. 30, 1733 ; d. July 21, 1734.,
31. *Isaac*, bap. July 6, 1735 ; d. Oct. 1, 1736.

IV. 10.–14. JOHN FITTS and HANNAH BOSWORTH, both of Ipswich, were published, Aug. 20, 1726, where she died, Apr. 17, 1765.

"Mr. JOHN FITTS and the WIDº. Susanna Hale, both of Ipswich, entered their intention of marriage, May 29th, 1779." She died, Mar. 22, 1787. He was a shoemaker and tanner, and either gave or received deeds, 1753, May 2 ; 1767, Jan. 27 ; 1768, Feb. 25. He died, Apr. 19, 1787. His Will was dated, Aug. 18, 1786, and presented for Probate, May 7, 1787 ; Inventory, Aug. 4, 1787 ; account of administration, Nov. 4, 1788 ; final account, June 8, 1790 ; division of the estate, June 29, 1790.

Children of John and Hannah (Bosworth) Fitts:
32. *Abigail*, d. Dec. 18, 1729.
† 33. *Moses*, bap. Oct. 25, 1730 ; d. Aug. 19, 1774.
34. *George*, bap. July 15, 1733 ; d. Aug. 11. 1733.
35. *John*, d. June 24, 1736.
36. *Isaac*, bap. Apr. 2, 1738 ; d. July 13, 1738.
† 37. *Josiah*, bap. July 22, 1739 ; m. Bethia Boardman.
38. *Sarah*, bap. Jan. 19, 1740 ; m. Peter Low of Newbury.
† 39. *Aaron*, bap. Feb. 6, 1742 ; m. Abigail Newman.
† 40. *Andrew*, bap. Apr. 1, 1744 ; d. Jan. 12, 1788.
41 *John*, bap. May 6, 1750.

IV. 10.–16. JEREMIAH FITTS and ELISABETH HASKELL, both of Ipswich, were published, Feb. 22, 1733. She was the daughter of Deacon Mark Haskell. He was a sadler, and transfers of land between himself and others took place in 1748, Oct. 24 ; 1753, Apr. 1 ; 1767, Mar. 7. He died, Feb. 3, 1801 ; a. 93. His Will dated Nov. 22, 1790, was presented for Probate, Mar. 12, 1801 ; Inventory and appraisement, Mar. 28, 1801 ; additional account, May 7, and Dec. 10, 1802 ; whole amount of estate, $1759.53 ; debts, $486.98.

Their children were :
42. *Jeremiah*, bap. Feb. 2. 1735 ; d. July 7, 1736.
43. *Jeremiah*, bap. Feb. 29, 1736 ; d. July 7, 1736.
† 44. *Mark*, bap. July 24, 1737 ; twice married.
45. *Jeremiah*, bap. Feb. 21, 1739.
46. *Elisabeth*, bap. Nov. 8, 1741 ; was admitted into full communion with the First Church, Ipswich, Oct. 4, 1761, and m. Nehemiah Haskall.

47. *Nathaniel,* bap. Mar. 3, 1744 ; d. Aug. 8, 1745.
48. *Abigail,* bap. Apr. 27, 1746.
† 49. *Nathaniel,* bap. May 30, 1747.
† 50. *Jeremiah,* bap. Oct. 29, 1749 ; m. Ruth Souther of Ipswish.
51. *Abigail,* bap. May 10, 1752.
52. *Hannah,* bap. Sep. 30, 1753 ; admitted to full communion with the church under the pastoral care of Rev. Levi Frisbie, Apr. 26, 1778 ; d. unm., Apr. 10, 1837.
53. *Eunice,* m. Ebenezer Safford of Ipswish, Apr. 2, 1789, by Rev. Levi Frisbie.

IV. 10.-20. "James Fitts and Wid° Mary Dutch, both of Ipswich, enter^d y^r intent° of marriage, July 6th, 1754."
Children baptized by Rev. John Walley, pastor of the Second church in Ipswich.
54. *Abigail,* bap. Mar. 30, 1755.
55. *Hannah,* bap. Oct. 24, 1756.
56. *Sarah,* bap. Jan. 1, 1758 ; d. unm., Dec. 1, 1828 ; a. 70, and Allen Putnam was appointed executor of her Will, July 1829.
57. *James,* bap. May 21, 1759.
58. *Mary,* bap. May, 15, 1763 ; m. Thomas Putnam, and had Allen b. Dec. 22, 1794, who m. Eliza Pope of Danvers, and was a Master mariner and admitted to Essex Lodge of Freemasons, Mar. 12, 1821.

FIFTH GENERATION.

V. 14.-33. "M^r· Moses Fitts and M^rs· Sarah Giddinge, both of Ipswich, entre^d y^r intent° of marriage, Dec^b 11th, 1756."
They were married, Feb. 10, 1757. Children, the first six, baptized by Rev. Nathaniel Royers.
59. *Sarah,* bap. Feb. 12, 1758 ; d. in infancy.
60. *Sarah,* bap. Nov. 16, 1760.
61. *John,* bap. 29 and b. 27, Aug. 1762.
62. *Hannah,* bap. June 3, 1764.
63. *Moses,* bap. Mar. 9, 1766.
64. *Bethia,* bap. Feb. 14, 1768 ; admitted to full communion with the First church in Ipswich by Rev. Levi Frisbie, Oct. 27, 1799.
65. *Elisabeth,* bap. Jan. 7, 1770.
66. *Eunice,* bap. Nov. 10, 1771 ; d. June 1, 1773.
67. *David,* b. July 19, and bap. July 22, 1774.
Moses Fitts was a tanner, and died intestate at Ipswich, Aug. 19, 1774. His widow was appointed administratrix, Sep. 26, 1774. Inventory returned in part, Mar. 9, 1775 ; in full, May 5, 1777. Whole amount 331£. 7s. 2¼d. Debts, 26£. 9s. 3d.
Right of Dower set off, June 7, 1776. The widow Sarah Fitts after the death of her first husband married Abraham Knowlton, Jr., of Ipswich, pub. Aug. 23, 1775.

V. 14.-37. "M^r· Josiah Fitts and M^rs· Bethiah Bordman, both of Ipswich, entred y^r intent° marriage, Dec^r· 16, 1775."

He was a tanner and received a deed of upland in Ipswich from Daniel Safford, July 9, 1767. He died intestate, and John Fitts and Bethia Fitts were appointed administrators, Nov. 4. 1776. Thirds set off to the widow, June 2, 1777, who married John Gould, Jr., of Topsfield, June 3, 1777, by Rev. Manassah Cutler of "Chebacco."

———

V. 14.–39. "Mr. Aaron Fitts and Mrs. Abigail Newman of Ipswich, entre^d y^r inten^o marriage, Novr. 28th. 1772."

Mr. Fitz settled in Ipswich as a "Cordwainer," but about the year 1794, removed on to a farm in Derry, N. H., which he purchased, Oct. 28, 1794, of Matthew Clark for "222 pds. lawful money." He sold his "land and buildings" in Ipswich to Nathaniel Baker, Nov. 6, 1794. Letters of administration on his estate were granted to his son, Aaron Fitz, Dec. 5, 1805. Inventory returned, Apr. 16, 1806. Amount, $1477.21. Appraisal of two thirds of the estate, Dec. 18, 1809.

Aaron Fitz of Gloucester was appointed administrator on the estate of his mother, Abigail Fitz, Dec. 19, 1818. Inventory returned, Jan. 4, 1820.

Children of Aaron and Abigail (Newman) Fitz:

68.   *Abigail*, m. James Miltemore of Londonderry, N. H., and lived at Andover, Vt.

† 69.   *Aaron*, b. Apr. 3, and bap. Apr. 12, 1778, at Ipswich.

70.   *Hannah*, bap. July 18, 1799; m. Ebenezer Stickney of Londonderry, and d. 1863; a. 83, leaving Aaron F.; John F.; Mary P.; Abbie F., m. Leonard Brickett; Elisabeth, m. her cousin William Fitz (104); Sarah A. W.

71.   *Mary*, bap. Feb. 24, 1782; unm.; d. 1863; a. 81. Her Will dated at Derry, Apr. 28, 1863, and allowed, May 20, 1863; mentions her "nephew, Aaron F. Stickney," and "neice, Mary P. Stickney," who was appointed "sole executrix."

72.   *John*, bap. June 29, 1783; m. Elisabeth, dau. of Capt. John White of the Revolution, and was drowned, leaving Aaron, Abigail and Mary, who lived in Gloucester, Mass.

73.   *George*, bap. Sep. 11, 1784; was twice married, and had one daughter, Ann Stickney, who d. leaving no children.

———

V. 14.–40. "Andrew Fitts and Phebe Lakeman, both of Ipswich, entred their intention of marriage, June 1, 1782."

They were married, June 20, 1782, and had only one child:

† 74.   *Josiah*, b. Dec. 9, 1783; m. Mary Poland.

Mr. Fitts was so injured in the head by falling from his horse as to become insane, and died, Jan. 12, 1788. Letters of administration were granted to Barnabas Dodge, June 8, 1790. Account of appraisers, Sept. 7, and of administrator, Dec. 6, 1790.

———

V. 16.–44. "Mr. Mark Fitts and Mrs. Elisabeth Campbell, both of Ipswich, entered their intention of marriage, Oc^{t.} 24th. 1759." They were married, Nov. 7, 1759, and settled in Newburyport, Mass. She was born at New Castle, Nov. 13, 1740, and died at Newburyport, Feb. 3, 1796.

Second marriage: Mark Fitz and Judith Richards, both of Newburyport, were married by Rev. Daniel Dana, D. D., Dec. 18, 1796. She died, Nov. 7, 1836 ; a. 87, leaving a Will dated, Sep. 12, 1818, which appointed Samuel Newman, Esq., executor, and was presented for Probate the third Tuesday of Dec. 1836.

Mark Fitz, Esq., was town clerk of Newburyport for many years, beside holding other important offices. "In 1758, he was a soldier and fought against the French and Savages. He was on the Committee of Safety during the Revolution, and afterward was in the State Legislature." He died, Oct. 20, 1812. His Will dated, July 3, 1812, mentions his wife, Judith, and sons, Nathaniel, Samuel, Henry, John, Aaron and William, and was admitted to Probate, Dec. 11, 1812. Account of administration entered, Dec. 10, 1813. Inventory presented, Nov. 20, 1815. Amount, $2797.00.

Children of Mark and Elisabeth Campbell Fitz :

75. *Jeremiah*, b. Sep. 23, 1760 ; d. at Newburyport, Oct. 8, 1781 ; a. 21.

† 76. *John*, b. Nov. 19, 1763 ; d. at Rye, New York, Aug. 12, 1846 ; a. 88.

77. *Nathaniel*, b. Aug. 20, 1765 ; m. Phebe ——— and had Charles who was b. Sep. 11, 1807, and d. Jan. 11, 1808.

78. *Isaac*, b. Sep. 3, 1767 ; d. at Newburyport, Aug. 28, 1800; a. 33.

† 79. *William*, b. Jan. 21, 1770 ; d. at New Orleans, Oct. 25, 1827 ; a. 58.

† 80. *Aaron*, b. Feb. 2, 1773 ; d. at Portland, Me.; May 10, 1813 ; a. 40.

81. *Samuel*, b. July 15, 1777 ; d. at Newburyport, Nov. 15, 1812 ; a. 35 ; letters of administration being granted to John Fitz, Mar. 5, 1813.

82. *Jeremiah*, b. Apr. 7, 1783 ; d. at Newburyport, Mar. 28, 1797 ; a. 14.

† 83. *Henry*, b. Jan. 17, 1785 ; d. at Baltimore, Md.

———

V. 16.–49. Nathaniel Fitz married Sarah ——— and lived in Danvers, Ipswich, and in Haverhill, Mass , where he was an householder, May 6, 1796.

Conveyances of land between him and others bear the dates, 1782, Aug. 8 ; 1790, June 8, and Dec. 22. He connected himself with the First Church, Ipswich, by letter from Danvers, Feb. 26, 1783, and in 1788, was a subscriber for Osterwald's Christian Theology.

Children: the first three baptized by Rev. Messrs. Holt and Prescott of Salem, middle precinct, afterward South Danvers.

84. *Nathaniel;* bap. Oct. 27, 1771.

85. *Ezekiel*, bap. Dec. 4, 1774.

86. *Sarah*, bap. Dec. 7, 1777.

87. *Jeremiah*, bap. Apr. 23, 1780.

88. *Jeremiah*, bap. June 16, 1782.

89. *Elisabeth*, bap. Oct. 5, 1788.

V. 16.–50. JEREMIAH FITZ married RUTH SOUTHER of Ipswich, who was born, Feb. 22, 1757, and died at Newburyport, Dec. 1825. Her Will dated at Newburyport, Aug. 18, 1825, and making her son, Leonard, sole executor, was presented for Probate the first Tuesday in Feb. 1826.

Jeremiah Fitz was a sadler, and lived in Ipswich, Londonderry, N. H., Haverhill and Bradford, Mass., where he died, June 25, 1804. Letters of administration were granted to Ruth Fitz, July 3, 1804, and and Inventory was returned, Oct. 2, 1804.

Their children were:

90. *Nathaniel*, b. at Ipswich, May 24, 1775; d. at Boston, Dec. 5, 1823, leaving Charles; d. in infancy. Sophronia; m. first, ―――― Hutton; second, ―――― Walsh. Mary; m. ―――― Lovejoy, and had four sons: George H., Charles F., Edwin A., Abram L.

91. *Jeremiah*, b. at Ipswich, Aug. 27, 1777; d. at Haverhill, July 23, 1787.

92. *Eunice*, b. at Ipswich, May 29, 1779; m. ―――― Payson, and d. at Bradford, Dec. 1845.

93. *Betsey*, b. at Londonderry, N. H., Mar. 19, 1781; m. ―――― Bartlett, and d. at Bangor, Me., May 3, 1862.

94. *John*, b. at Londonderry, Apr. 24, 1783, and was lost at sea.

95. *Rebecca*, b. at Haverhill, Nov. 7, 1786; m ―――― Davis, and d. at Newburyport, Mar. 31, 1855.

96. *Polly*, b. at Haverhill, Dec. 16, 1789; m. ―――― Clement, and d. at Newburyport, Jan. 1, 1848.

97. *Joanna*, b. at Haverhill, July 31, 1791, and d. at West Newbury, Nov. 16, 1840.

† 98. *Jeremiah*, b. at Haverhill, Dec. 17, 1793; m. Hannah Eaton, Dec. 25, 1817.

† 99. *William*, b. at Haverhill, Jan. 10, 1797, and d. at Salisbury, Apr. 28, 1843; a. 46.

100. *Sophia*, b. at Haverhill, Aug. 17, 1799; m. ―――― Haskall, and d. at Newburyport, Dec. 17, 1816.

† 101. *Leonard*, b. at Haverhill, Nov. 9, 1802, and d. at Pembroke, N. H., Oct. 1842.

SIXTH GENERATION.

VI. 39.–69. AARON FITZ married NANCY RIGGS, 1803. She was born in Gloucester, July 28, 1776, the grand daughter of Rev. John Rogers of Gloucester, and descended from John Rogers the martyr at Smithfield. Aaron Fitz, Esq., settled at Gloucester, but died at Manchester, Mass., July 31, 1861; a. 83.

Their children were:

102. *Nancy*, d. in infancy.

† 103. *Charles*, b. July 2, 1806; m. Betsey B. Day, July 3, 1831, the grand daughter of Rev. B. Bradstreat. He resided in Gloucester and represented the town in General Court in 1864 and 1865, besides holding many other civil offices. No children.

† 104. *William F.*, b. Dec. 16, 1808; settled in Manchester, Mass, as a manufacturer of furniture, and Jan. 22, 1868, was chosen delegate to Washington by the Manufacturer's Convention of New England as-

sembled at Worcester. He married first, Eunice C. Baker, Dec. 15, 1833, by whom he had four children who d. in infancy, and Eunice Augusta, b. May 22, 1845. After. the death of his first wife in 1848, he m. Elisabeth Stickney, his cousin, Apr. 2, 1850, by whom he had Charles William, Sep. 10, 1853, and Mary Elisabeth, Apr. 27, 1857.

† 105. *Alfred,* b. May 30, 1811 ; m. Elisabeth Allen, and d. Apr. 17, 1845. Their children were : Nancy, b. Jan. 1845 ; d. Apr. 6, 1853, and three others who d. in infancy.

106. *Nancy,* b. Aug. 30, 1814 ; d. Nov. 19, 1834.

107. *Aaron,* b. June 24, 1817 ; d. Nov. 16, 1843.

––––––

VI. 40.–74. JOSIAH FITZ and MARY POLAND, both of Ipswich, were married, Nov. 26, 1807. She was born, Aug. 22, 1788, and died, Feb. 27, 1858. They lived in Beverly and Salem.

Their children were :

† 108. *Daniel Poland,* b. at Beverly, Aug. 13, 1808 ; m. first, Martha Radford, June 8, 1831, by Rev. Mr. Willis. She was the dau. of John and Martha Radford of Salem. Her children were : Daniel R., b. Oct. 14, 1834, and wrecked on board of the Prairie Flower in Boston Harbor, June 8, 1858 ; and several other children who d. in infancy. He m. second, Sarah Ellen Brown, June 15, 1843, by Rev. Charles Mason of St. Peter's church, Salem. She was the dau. of James and Phebe Brown of Salem. Her children were : Hellen Johnson, b. Oct. 29, 1844 ; m. Albert Towle, July 12, 1864, and d. Jan. 30, 1866, leaving a son Charles, b. Jan. 29, 1866. Eliza Ann, b. June 1, 1846. Margarett Blanchard, b. Aug. 9, 1847. Andrew, b. Sep. 27, 1850. Daniel P. Fitz, Esq., served on the board of aldermen at Salem, and was clerk of the Overseers of the Poor for ten years previous to 1866.

† 109. *Josiah,* b. at Beverly, May 26, 1811 ; m. Sarah Rachel, the dau. of Andrew and Rachel (Safford) Morgan of Salem, b. July 15, 1809. He was a baker, and lived in Salem, Boston, Gloucester, Lynn and Chelsea. Their children were : Mary Augusta, Mar. 29, 1830 ; m. James H. Short of Atkinson, N. H., Oct 14, 1857, and afterward, Daniel N. Hoit of Sandown, N. H. Josiah, Oct. 26, 1831 ; m. Mary Ann Hillar of Marblehead, and had Henry Eugene ; Josiah, 4th ; Anna Barnes ; Luella. Andrew Morgan, Apr. 5, 1833 ; d. Aug. 29, 1833. Elisabeth Davenport, July 21, 1834 ; m. Francis Rounds, and had Josiah and Frank Everett. Henry, Feb. 10, 1837 ; m. Frances Abbie Stewart of Boston, and had Ina Frances. Sarah Rachel, Nov. 19, 1838 ; m. William Sawyer of Limmington, Me., and had Wm. Frederick. Clara Morgan, Apr 8, 1840. Frederick, Oct. 16, 1842. Eugene, Dec. 31, 1844 ; d. Sep. 8, 1845. Eliza Ann, Feb. 26, 1846 ; d. Mar. 12, 1846. Anna Jane, Apr. 30, 1850.

110. *Andrew,* b. Nov. 1815, at Beverly, and was drowned at sea, 1841 ; a. 26.

111. *Francis Larkin,* d. young.

† 112. *Joseph Lamson,* b. Nov. 1819 ; a seaman and ship carpenter ; m. Hannah Fiske Pinkham of Salem, and had Harriet ; Joseph Warren ; George Ware.

113. *Mary Jane,* b. Jan. 19, 1822 ; a successful teacher at Salem.

114. *John Meade*, d. in infancy.
115. *Eliza Ann*, b. Oct. 20, 1827 ; d. Feb. 24, 1845.
116. *George Henry*, b. Jan. 8, 1830.; d. Aug. 1831.

VI. 44.-76. JOHN FITZ and SARAH PERKINS, both of Ipswich, were married, Nov. 16, 1791, by Rev. Levi Frisbie.

Mr. Fitz settled in Newburyport where he was a Justice of the Peace and Quorum, and Town Clerk from about 1805 to 1812, and again from 1819 to 1830.. He united with the North church under the pastoral care of Rev. Samuel Spring, and his wife united with the First church in Ipswich, Sep. 13, 1789. Mr. Fitz removed to the city of New York in 1831, and died at Rye, West Chester Co., Aug. 12, 1846 ; a. 83. Mr. George Lunt of. the Boston Courier, once wrote the following pungent epigram upon him :

> "Rome may boast of her heroes,
> 　Greece her wits,
> Briton her naval chiefs,
> 　And we our Fitz."

Their children were :
117. *John*, b. Oct. 10 ; bap. Oct. 21, 1792 ; d. age about 21.
118. *Sally*, b. July 6, 1796 ; d. June 9, 1825.
119. *Isaac*, b. Nov. 30, 1798 ; d. Oct. 2, 1802.
120. *Hannah*, b. Sep. 7, 1801 ; unm.
121. *Mary*, b. Dec. 1806 ; unm.
122. *Abigail*, b. Feb. 20, 1810 ; unm.
123. *Isaac*, settled in New York.
124. *Jeremiah*, settled in New York.

VI. 44.-79. WILLIAM FITZ of Portsmouth, and ANNA STONE, were married, Oct. 18, 1795, by Rev. Thomas Carey of Newburyport. She was born, Sep. 29, 1772, and died at Newburyport, Apr. 5, 1845 He died at New Orleans, Oct. 25, 1827.

Their children were :
125. *William*, b. at Portsmouth, July 31, 1796 ; m. and d. at New Orleans, Feb. 19, 1835.
126. *Elisabeth*, b. at Portsmouth, Sep. 11, 1797 ; d. at Newburyport, Oct. 10, 1798.
127. *Mark*, b. at Newburyport, Mar. 19, 1799 ; d. at New Orleans, Mar. 29, 1837.
† 128. *George*, b. at Newburyport, Feb. 16, 1801 ; m. Lucy Ann Leslie of Newburyport, June 25, 1826, by Rev. Luther F. Dimmick, D. D. Their children were : Anna Stone, May 16, 1827 ; a successful teacher. Mary Elisabeth, Sep. 15, 1828 ;.m. Jonathan Bickford, Captain of the Monte Christo, and who d. at sea, 1865, on the coast of Africa. Lucy, Mar. 12, 1832 ; d. July 10, 1839. George Edward, d. in infancy, July 18, 1830. Franklin, Oct. 9, 1834 ; m. Mary Wells Blake, Feb. 29, 1859. Ellen, Dec. 30, 1836 ; m. John Cross. Philip, Feb. 2, 1841,

who with his brother Franklin entered the business of Ship Broker and Commission Merchant, Boston, under the title "Philip Fitz & Co."

129. *Charles*, b. at Portland, Apr. 23, 1803 ; d. at New Orleans, Sep. 1, 1820.

† 130. *Albert*, b. at Boston, July 11, 1809 ; m. at Boston, Sep. 7, 1833, Eliza Roberts Leighton, born Nye, dau. of Allen Nye at Sandwich, Dec. 21, 1811. Albert Fitz was a private clerk of Hon. Daniel Webster, and merchantile agent of the United States to the West Indies, and d. at Aux Cayes, July 22, 1852. After the death of her husband Mrs. Fitts became Principal of a Family School at Brookline, Mass. Their children were: Eliza Roberts, July 5, 1834. Albert, Apr. 28, 1836. Walter Scott, Mar. 23, 1838. Francis, May 15, 1840. Reginald Heber, May 5, 1843 ; enlisted in the 44th Reg. Mass Vol. ; a graduate of Harvard Médical College Edith, Feb. 10, 1845. Charles, May 2, 1847 ; d. Mar. 30, 1851.

131. *Sarah Ann*, b. at Boston, Nov. 24, 1810 ; d. at Boston, Nov. 7, 1811.

VI. 44.–80. AARON FITZ married REBECCA WARREN, Oct. 19, 1806, by Rev. Samuel Deane, D. D., of Portland, Me., and died at Portland, May 10, 1813 ; a. 40.

The children :

132. *Elisabeth.*

133. *Rebecca.*

VI. 44.–83. " Mr. HENRY FITZ and SUSAN BRADLEY PAGE, both of Newburyport," were married, Jan. 29, 1807. This was by the Rev. Samuel Spring, D. D.

Their children were :

134. *Henry*, b. at Newburyport, Dec. 31, 1808 ; a celebrated teles-cope maker in the city of New York. At the time of his death he was engaged in making a twenty-four inch telescope, the pride of our later observatories.

135. *Susan.*

VI. 50.–98. JEREMIAH FITZ married HANNAH EATON, Dec. 25, 1817. She was born, Mar. 11, 1799, the daughter of Jesse and Hannah (Smith) Eaton of Plaistow, N. H. He lived at Haverhill, Chelsea and Newburyport. While at Haverhill, he was a Deacon of the First Baptist church over which his son, Rev. William Fitz, was afterward installed pastor.

Their children were seven sons :

136. *Jesse E.*, b. at Haverhill, Dec. 31, 1818, and d. June 2, 1822.

137. *Richard H.*, b. Mar. 16, 1821 ; d. about 1857.

138. *Jesse E.*, b. May 11, 1823 ; d. 1861.

139. *Eustace Carey*, b. Oct. 15, 1825, and was drowned, May 14, 1829.

† 140. *William*, b. Aug. 5, 1828 ; m. Ellen S. Salisbury, Aug. 26, 1857, by Rev. James B. Simmons. She was born, Apr. 16, 1836, at

Providence, R. I., the daughter of Daniel M., and Emeline E. Salisbury. Rev. William Fitz was settled over the Baptist church in Westerly, R. I., and also in Hartford, Ct., and in 1866 over the First Baptist church in Haverhill, Mass. Their children were: William Ernest, June 9, 1856. Arthur Salisbury, Mar. 24, 1860. Edward Eustace, Aug. 23, 1862. Howard Whittier, Mar. 6, 1866.

† 141. *Eustace C.*, b. Feb. 5, 1833; m. Sarah Jane Blanchard, Jan. 10, 1856. She was b. Oct. 22, 1835, the daughter of Alfred and Margarett (Cluly) Blanchard of Belfast, Me. Her mother was descended from the distinguished settlers of Londonderry, N. H. Hon. E. C. Fitz, Esq., was Mayor of Chelsea, Mass., in 1863, 1864, 1865. During the Rebellion, he greatly distinguished himself for his prompt loyalty and shrewd judicial ability. He was a Vice-President of the Republican State Convention at Worcester, Sep. 14, 1865. For many years he was Superintendent of the Baptist Sabbath School, and in 1866, was chosen President of the Young Men's Christian Association at Chelsea. Their children were: Frank Eustace, Nov. 14, 1857. Emma Jennie, Oct. 17, 1859. Alfred William, May 4, 1862.

142. *Samuel Eaton*, b. Jan. 26, 1836; a graduate of Harvard College, 1862, and of Newton Theological Seminary.

VI. 50.–99. WILLIAM FITZ and ELEANOR HARDY, both of Newburyport, were married, May 4, 1829, by the Rev. Charles W. Milton. He died at Salisbury, intestate, Apr. 28, 1843; a. 43. A committee to appraise his estate, and an administrator were appointed, Sep. 13, 1845. She afterward m. Daniel T. Tucker of Newbury; pub. Nov. 14, 1845.

The children of William and Eleanor Fitz were:

143. *William Henry*, b. Dec. 22, 1829, at Newburyport, where he was for many years a constable and connected with the board of police.

144. *Abby Ann*, b. June 4, 1840, at Salisbury.

VI. 50.–101. LEONARD FITZ and SARAH BROWN, both of Newburyport, were married, Sep. 20, 1826, by Rev. Daniel Dana, D. D. She was the daughter of Ebenezer Brown, and born in Raymond, N. H. After the death of Mr. Fitz, which occurred at Pembroke, N. H., Jan. 15, 1841, she married Thomas Dresser at Salisbury, Mass., Sep. 5, 1844, who died at Haverhill, June 8, 1846. She died at Lowell, June 30, 1850.

The children of Leonard and Sarah Fitz were:

† 145. *John*, b. at Newburyport, June 21, 1827; m. Mrs. Abbie Fifield, (m. n. Beau), Apr. 17, 1852. He settled in Candia, N. H., and wrote his name John Edmund Fitts to distinguish himself from others of the family bearing the same name. He was an ingenious mechanic and the Patentee of Fitts' Centre Balance Gate. Their children were: Sarah Jane, Feb. 15, 1854. Abbie Lucinda, Aug. 6, 1856.

146. *Sarah Ann*, b. at Newburyport, Dec. 2. 1828; m. at Nashua, N. H., Nov. 22, 1849, to George E. Hayward, and lived in Lowell,

where he d. Nov. 27, 1854 ; a. 27.   She had children : Luella T., Oct. 6, 1850 ; d. Aug. 11, 1851.   George Albert, Sep. 2, 1852, adopted by Justus Richardson of Dracut, Mass., and died at Lowell, Mar. 28, 1856 ; a. 27.

147.   *Charles William*, b. at Newburyport, Aug 6, 1830 ; unm. ; d in Australia, Oct. 10, 1863 ; a. 33.

148.   *Mary Jane*, b. at Epping, N. H., Dec. 14, 1835; m. at Boston, Aug. 25, 1858, to Henry U. York, Esq., lived in Winchester, and had Mary Isabella, May 19, 1859.

6

Bristol County Branch.

FOURTH GENERATION.

IV. 5.–11. "ABRAHAM FITTS and PHEBE FULLER, both of Ipswich, were published the third day of March, 1721–22." She died Aug. 25, 1739, and he married a second time. "ABRAHAM FITTS and ELIZ ͣ CROSS, widow, both of Ipswich, ent ͩ their intent° of marriage, Nov ᵇ· 18 ᵗʰ 1739."

Deeds of land passed between Abraham Fitts and others, 1714, Jan. 20 ; 1728, Jan. 24 ; 1731, June 13 and Nov. 2. In 1736, he received a quit-claim deed from his brothers and sisters of their "interest in a Narragansett Right which was derived by our honored father, Mr. Abraham Fitts, deceased, late of Ipswich, which Right is in the township of Salen called Hegany, county of Middlesex."

"A list of the members of the First Chh. of Christ in Ipswich taken Apr. 21, 1746, by Nath ͪ Rogers Pastor," has the following names :
Jeremiah Fitts and his wife.
Abraham Fitts and his wife.
Isaac Fitts.
Robert Fitts.
Wife of John Fitts.
"Admitted to full communion since y ͤ y ͬ 1739."
1742, June 12, John Fitts.
1743, Jan. 9, John Fitts.
"Abraham Fitts, husbandman," died June 1763. His Will dated, Nov. 20, 1757, with a codicil, was admitted to Probate, July 11, 1763.
The children of Abraham and Phebe Fitts were :

    12. *Abraham,* bap. Sep. 29, 1723 ; d. Oct. 3, 1727.
† 13. *Daniel,* bap. May 2, 1725 ; m. Christianna Smith.
    14. *Phebe,* bap. Oct. 6, 1728 ; m. —— Achus.
    15. *Mary,* bap. Feb. 1,. 1730 ; m. —— Gordan.
    16. *Abraham,* bap. Jan. 23, 1732 ; d. Sep. 30, 1736.
    17. *James,* bap. July 7, 1734 ; d. May 20, 1736.
    18. *Sarah,* bap. Mar. 21, 1736.
    19. *Abraham,* d. Apr. 11, 1738.

FIFTH GENERATION.

V. 11.–13. "DANIEL FITTS and CHRISTIANNA SMITH, both of Ipswich, entered y^r intention of marriage. Dec^{b.} 15th. 1750."

Mr. Fitts united with the First church in Ipswich the following year. Tradition says he suddenly dropped dead in his field in the time of the Revolution.

The children were :

† 20. *Daniel*, m. Elisabeth Fuller.

21. *Abraham*, bap. Nov. 26, 1753 ; moved to Maine and was not heard of afterward.

† 22. *Moses*, b. May 18 and bap. Dec. 28, 1755.

23. *Eunice*, bap. Apr. 23, 1758 ; d. young.

† 24. *Israel*, bap. Dec. 30, 1759.

‡ 25. *Stephen*, bap. Apr. 11, 1762.

26. *Solomon*, "D^{a.} of Danl Fitts, baptiz^d March 18th. 1763."

27. *James*, bap. Sep. 8, 1765 ; m. —— Messer of Methuen, and settled in Leicester, Vt. No children except by adoption.

† 28. *David*, b. July 1, and bap. July 18, 1767.

29. *Lydia*, died young.

SIXTH GENERATION.

VI. 13.–20. DANIEL FITTS married ELISABETH FULLER of Ashford, Conn. He was a farmer and settled in Ashford in the time of the Revolution, 1777.

Their children were :

† 30. *Daniel*, b. Nov. 30, 1776 ; m. Abigail Slade, 1806, and settled in Pomfret, Ct., where he had issue: Reuben, Apr. 30, 1808 ; unm. Lucius, June 29, 1810 ; m. Adalaide Tucker of Pomfret. Lyman, Jan. 22, 1815 ; m. Harriet M. Richards of Ashford. Emily, Jan. 31, 1823 ; m. James W. Manning of Pomfret, May 6, 1846.

† 31. *Ebenezer Fuller*, b. Dec. 23, 1778 ; m. Nancy Chaffee, 1803 ; settled in Eastford, Ct., and had issue : Mary, m. James H. Butler of Springfield, Mass. Almira, b. 1805 ; m. Joseph J. Carpenter of Hartford, Ct., and d. 1847. Nancy, m. Jason Rhodes of Townsend, Vt. George, b. Jan. 1810 ; a boot and shoe manufacturer at Bristol, R. I. ; m. Delany Williston of Tiverton, and had George Frederick, Mar. 25, 1839 ; Thomas Fisher, Apr. 22, 1842 ; Susan Catharine, June 17, 1844 ; Henry Martyn, June 24, 1846 ; Almira B., Jan. 17, 1848 ; Joseph Francis, Aug. 5, 1850 ; d. Apr. 2, 1857 ; Delany Melissa, Mar. 17, 1852 ; William James, Nov. 12, 1853 ; d. July 9, 1855 ; Lucian, Nov. 9, 1855 ; Patience Emma, Dec. 7, 1856 ; Annie Frances, Dec. 25, 1859 ; A daughter, May 3, 1862. Frederick, b. Apr. 1813 ; unm. Susan, b. July, 1816. Joseph, d. with small pox. Lewis Francis, b. Jan. 1822 ; unm.

32. *Benjamin*, b. Nov. 30, 1780, and d. previous to 1863.

33. *Elisabeth*, b. May 12, 1783 ; unm ; d. May, 1862.

34. *Duty*, b. Mar. 18, 1785 ; twice m. and d. 1869.

35. *Rhoda*, b. May 27, 1787 ; unm.

VI. 13.-22. MOSES FITTS, with several of his brothers, enlisted in the Army during the War of Independence, where he remained till its close. He then moved to West Hartford, Ct., where he married DOROTHY BELDEN, a native of that town, 1785. She was born, Jan. 9, 1757, and died Jan 9, 1825 ; a. 68. Soon after the birth of their eldest child they moved to the vicinity of Johnston, Fulton County, N. Y., then a wilderness. After residing in New York about five years, the Indians became troublesome, and they were forced to return to West Hartford. He died May 18, 1815 ; a. 60.

They had nine children who remained a family unbroken by death as late as 1862.

36. *Eunice*, b. June 20, 1787; m. Joseph Hart, and had nine children.

37. *Dorothy*, b. 1788 ; d. Oct. 4, 1863 ; m. Jeremiah Wilcox of West Hartford, and had issue : Mary Ann, m. Wm. W. Flagg, and Caroline, m. Milton Braman.

† 38. *Sylvester*, b. Feb. 28, 1790 ; thrice m. ; first, to Nancy Wells of Huntington, Ct., May 10, 1812, who d. at East Windsor, Jan. 23, 1827 ; a. 34; by whom he had issue : Mary Jane, d. ; a. 12. Emeline R , d. in infancy. Sylvester W., Aug. 17, 1816 ; m. Levia M. Hart, Apr. 14, 1842; settled in Gustavus, Ohio, and had Emily Jane ; Almira L.; Melvin H. ; Josephine M. Phebe A., Sep. 5, 1818 ; m. George W. White of Cazenovia, N. Y., 1841. Emeline R., June 19, 1820 ; m. Lucius W. Case of Gustavus, 1844, and d. Dec. 27, 1866. Edward B., Nov. 8, 1822 ; m. Roxanna Cowden, and d. in Gustavus, Aug. 24, 1865, leaving William C.; Minnie M. ; Ella A.; Charles B. John F., Oct. 26, 1826, of East Windsor Hill, Ct., unm. Married second, Clarissa Wilcox of Avon, Ct., July 4, 1827, who d. Mar. 16, 1829, leaving no children. Married third, Emily S. Curtis of Farmington, Ct., Aug. 12, 1830, by whom he had : Harriet Eliza, Feb. 4, 1834. Charles Curtis, Sep. 13, 1835. Amzi Wilson, d. in infancy.

† 39. *John*, b. Feb. 22, 1792; m. Elisabeth Opp, Jan. 1, 1820, who was b. July 3, 1799, and d. Feb. 4, 1841. They resided in Dansville, N. Y., and had issue : John J., Oct. 15, 1822 ; m. Mary Ann Whiting, 1856. Eliza S., Sep. 6, 1824. Mary C., Sep. 11, 1826. Harriet A., May 28, 1828. Friend P., m. and settled in Brookline, N. Y. Dorothy A., Jan. 4, 1832. Edmund Henry, Feb. 1. 1834; d. Jan. 12, 1835. Ann Maria, Nov. 26, 1835 ; m. Stiles Treat of Orange, Ct.

40. *Sarah*, b. 1794 ; m. Leonard Braman of W. Hartford.

† 41. *David S.*, b. Apr. 3, 1795 ; m. Sophia Morton of East Windsor, Ct., May 24, 1820, and settled in Oberlin, Ohio. She was b. Nov. 18, 1793, and d. Sep. 24, 1864. He afterward m. Joanna Burnham of Waterbury, Ct., 1865. Children by Sophia were : David B., Mar. 27, 1821, of Illinois ; m. Rebecca Gibbs and had Morton, 1847; Elisabeth, 1849 ; Mary, 1851 ; William, 1853 ; Twins, Martha and Mary, d. in infancy. Elisabeth S., Dec. 7, 1822 ; d. Nov. 14, 1824. Leverett E., Apr. 6, 1826 ; d. Feb. 1, 1827. Leverett E., Jan. 7, 1828, and lived in Cincinnati. George W., May 14, 1830 ; a merchant in Oberlin ; m. Ellen Hill, and had Anna S., Nov. 24, 1853. Eveline A., Feb. 29, 1856. George Hamilton, Dec. 16, 1858. Emily Hammond, Nov. 15, 1862 ; d. Aug. 30, 1865. William Hill, Aug. 9, 1865. Mary J., Mar. 15, 1833 ; d. Dec. 17, 1833. Henry M., Nov. 16, 1835 ; a merchant in Leslie, Mich. ; m. Caroline More.

† 42. *James,* b. May 22, 1798; m. first Betsey Shelton Hubbell, Apr. 19, 1821, who d. Aug. 3, 1857, and second, Harriet Augusta (Shelton) Waters, Nov. 3, 1858. He was a woolen manufacturer and lived in Huntington, Stratford and Orange, Ct. Children by his first wife: Mary Ann, Dec. 8, 1823; d. Apr. 1, 1824. John James, Feb. 7, 1826; d. Oct. 3, 1842. George Washington, Mar. 17, 1831; d. Nov. 27, 1832.

† 43. *Harvey,* b. June 10, 1801; m. Mary Gilbert of Huntington, Ct., Mar. 11, 1824, and lived in Orange, Ct., and Gustavus and Kingsville, Ohio. His children were: Curtis Harvey, Mar. 28, 1825; m. Margaret Bliss, May 2, 1864, and had Sophia, Mar. 15, 1865; Curtis Bliss, Apr. 10, 1866. Elisabeth Ann, Jan. 25, 1827; m. Fay S. Noyes, Dec. 16, 1852; d. Sep. 4, 1866, and had Myra Elisabeth, Nov. 9, 1854; Nora, Feb. 11, 1859; Arthur Fay, Feb. 28, 1863. Harriet Patience, Dec. 18, 1829; m. Francis A. Kinman, June 4, 1851. Lucy Maria, Mar. 16, 1833; m. John J. Stanton, Oct. 27, 1859, and had Harriet, Dec. 1860; Alice, Oct. 1862; Edward R., Oct. 1864; Annette, May, 1866. Lewis Gilbert, May 21, 1835; d. Oct. 10, 1851. Cornelia, June 21, 1837; d. Nov. 10, 1845. Mary Jane, Aug. 27, 1839; d. Oct. 3, 1851. Ellen, Jan. 22, 1842. An infant b. Jan. 3, and d. Feb. 25, 1846.

44. *Lydia,* b. July 22, 1804; m. Dec. 24, 1823, Lewis Gilbert who was b. Mar. 20, 1798. Their children were: Sarah Ann, July 19, 1826; d. Apr. 20, 1861. Emily Jane, Feb. 22, 1829; m. Perry Hall, Nov. 4, 1852. Almina Cornelia, Dec. 19, 1832; d. Oct. 21, 1850. Agur Lewis, Feb. 31, 1837; d. Aug. 9, 1838. David, Mar. 13, 1840; d. May 3, 1840. Frances Maria, Jan. 24, 1843; m. Thomas Ford, Nov. 11, 1863, who d. July 3, 1864.

VI. 13.–24. ISRAEL FITTS married SARAH COOK of Salisbury, Vt., where he settled as a farmer and died, 1815; a. 55.

Their children were:

† 45. *James,* b. Sep. 1786; m. Charlotte Grundie, and had issue: Eunice Sophronia, Dec. 22, 1809; m. William Carlisle. Sally Maria, May, 22, 1812; m. Franklin ———. David Grundie, July 29, 1815. James, Aug. 13, 1818; Constable of Salisbury, 1848, '9, '50, '51, '52, '53, '57, '58, '59. Charlotte, July 26, 1825. He was Selectman of Salisbury in 1847, '48, '49, '55, '56, and d. in the winter of 1864–5.

† 46. *Ansel,* resided at Cleaveland, Ohio, and m. first, Lovena Franklin, by whom he had issue: Mary Ann; Laura Lrancis. Married second, Cynthia Emerson, by whom he had: Ansel; Emerson; C. Maria.

47. *Nancy,* m. Edward Moren and d. Apr. 14, 1820, in her 32d year, leaving Cynthia Almena, who m. Chauncey King of Guilford, Vt.

48. *Sally,* m. Perley Enos of Leicester, Vt., who d. May 25, 1836, in his 54th year. Their chlderen were: Marcia, Dec. 18, 1811; m. John L. Marsh of Clarendon, Vt., Mar. 13, 1837. Horace L., Sep. 29, 1814; m. Mary Conant, Mar. 27, 1839, and moved to Lawrence, Kansas. Harriet, Aug. 2, 1816; m. Daniel G. Henry of W. Rochester, Vt., Dec. 31, 1840. Israel Fitts, Oct. 25, 1818; m. Mary Tupper, Sep.

29, 1840. Marion, Mar. 18, 1822; m. Alvah S. Larabee, Feb. 24, 1841, and d. Feb. 10, 1842. Sarah Cook, Dec. 26, 1825; m. George F. Wheeler, Dec. 25, 1849, and moved to Wisconsin. Nancy, Nov. 17, 1827; m. Hiram Capron. Charles, Feb. 23, 1830; went to California. Charlotte Augusta, Dec. 3, 1833.

49. *Harriet*, m. Elias Woodruff, settled in the State of New York, and had children: Joseph, Sarah A.; Harriet and Hannah.

50. *Laura*, d. young.

51. *Laura Ann*, m. Nov. 18, 1824, Rev. Samuel Sparhawk, Pastor of the Cong. church at West Randolph, Vt. Their children were three sons and five daughters: Mary Pricilla, Mar. 13, 1826; d. Mar. 14, 1829. George Enos. Feb. 20, 1829; a Homeopathic Physician at Gaysville, Vt. Luther T., Feb. 11, 1831; a Daguerreian Artist at West Randolph. Sarah Cook, Sep. 15, 1834; d. May 11, 1835. Martha Allyn, Feb. 15, 1837. Mary Adelaide, Aug. 2, 1839; d. Nov. 18, 1856. Samuel Henry, Dec. 11, 1842; a Physician. Sarah Ellen, Aug. 22, 1845.

VI. 13.–25. STEPHEN FITTS married POLLY KNOWLTON, and settled on a farm in Ashford, Ct., where he died, Feb. 16, 1840.

Their children were:

52. *Christianna*, b. Aug. 11, 1793; m. William Loomis, 1819, and had issue: Mary Ann, Jan. 29, 1820. Chester, Feb. 8, 1822.

† 53. *Stephen*, b. Oct. 29, 1798; m. Waitstill Moore, and settled on the homestead in Ashford, where his children were: Thomas Knowlton, Oct. 23, 1831. John Stephen, Mar. 12, 1839. George Henry, Apr. 17, 1840. Mary Catherine, Feb. 23, 1843.

54. *Maria*, b. July 18, 1802; m. William Mosely, and had Nathan James, Aug. 29, 1833, who m. Betsey Ames, Dec. 1859.

55. *Thomas*, b. July 11, 1807; d. Feb. 7, 1831.

VI. 13.–28. DAVID FITTS married DELIA BUCKLIN of Rehoboth, Mass., Feb. 8. 1795. She was from a distinguished family of nine children. Thomas an older brother was an eminent physician at Hopkinton, Mass., while her youngest brother, Sylvester F. Bucklin, was pastor of the First church of Marlboro', settled Nov. 2, 1808, dismissed June 20, 1832.

The following obituary notice was written by her pastor, Rev. J. O. Burney of Seekonk, Mass.

"The decease of this eminent mother in Israel deserves more than the mere notice that she died. She was the daughter of Mr. John Bucklin, and widow of the late Mr. David Fitts. She was born under the British crown, in Seekonk, Dec. 2, 1774, and died in the same place, April 29, 1861. From early childhood she was taught the truths of the Christian religion, which were of unspeakable comfort to her in after life. She in turn taught these same precious truths to her own children, and lived to see five of them, with their husbands and wives, and a number of her grand children, members of the same church with herself. Mrs. Fitts remembered the Sabbath, and reverenced the sanctuary, and no one was more constantly there, and no one more devout and happy. She loved the Sabbath school and Bible class, and to extreme old age, was a teacher in the one, or a member of the other. She was a lover of good people; a friend to mission, and to all humane and benevolent institutions; and proved her friendship by her liberal contributions, and by the provisions of her Will.

Though her mind was partially impaired by great age so as to be forgetful of worldly things, yet, the mention of the truths of the Bible, the name of Jesus, or the voice of prayer, would call out such expressions of joy as to convince all her friends that her knowledge of spiritual things and her love of them, were as when in the vigor of life. Her excellency of character and uniform piety greatly-endeared her to the church and people with whom she worshiped, by whom she will be long held in affectionate remembrance. 'The righteous shall be in everlasting remembrance.' She died as she lived, full of faith and of the Holy Ghost. Her end was peace.

Seekonk, June 2, 1861."

Here follows an obituary of Mr. Fitts.

"Died in Seekonk, May 18, 1846; Mr. David Fitts, son of Daniel and Christianna (Smith) Fitts, formerly of Ipswich, Mass., in his seventy-ninth year. For more than fifty years he was an inhabitant of Seekonk, where he sustained, by common consent, the reputation of a good neighbor, a good citizen, and an honest man. Mr. Fitts was a lover of the Sabbath, a constant attendant upon public worship, and, with a single exception, was present at the public services of the Annual Thanksgiving for more than fifty successive years. In infancy, he was dedicated to God by his parents in baptism, and, although the vows for their son lay long under the altar, yet they were not forgotten of God.

It is a singular fact, and often mentioned by the deceased with gratitude, that he had scarcely a day's sickness in all his life; and although he had nine children, no death had occurred in his family for more than half a century.

For some time past Mr. Fitts had indulged a hope of a glorious immortality through faith and grace. A short time before his death, he expressed his confidence and hope of a better world; and almost with his expiring breath, like Stephen, he committed his departing spirit into the hands of his Saviour saying, 'Lord Jesus, receive my spirit.'"

The following appropriate lines are engraved on his monument:

"Weep not for me—'Tis unkindness to weep,
The weary worn frame is but fallen asleep;
It sleeps now in Jesus! How sweet his repose!
No more of fatigue or endurance it knows."

The children of David and Delia (Bucklin) Fitts were:
56. *Almira*, b. Apr. 25, 1797; m. Joel Whitaker of Seekouk, Dec. 23, 1827, and had issue: Mary Ellen, Oct. 14, 1828. David Fitts, Feb. 27, 1831; m. Jan. 24, 1856, and had Emily Frances, Nov. 30, 1856, ob. Jan. 10, 1864; Walter Herbert, Dec. 8, 1858; Edward Everett, Sep. 1860; James Otis, Oct. 20, 1862; Lepha Ide, Dec. 31, 1864; Abbie Webber, Mar. 26, 1867. Nelson Bowen, Mar. 24, 1834;

a.Dentist in Providence, R. I. ; m. Mary Lizzie Salisbury of Warren,
May, 14, 1868. Benjamin Carpenter, Oct. 8, 1836 ; ob. Sep. 16, 1838.
Susan Harriet, June 12, 1840 ; m. William Ross of Providence, June
13, 1858, and had Sophia Peckham, Apr. 16, 1859 ; Alice Sophronia,
Nov. 24, 1861 ; Susan Aurelia, Oct. 2, 1862 ; William Abbott, Dec. 19,
1864 ; Grace Bucklin, Mar. 22, 1867.

† 57. *Albert*, b. Apr. 1, 1800 ; m. Triphosa Bartlett of Plymouth,
Mass., May, 1824, and settled as a carpenter at Central Falls, R. I.
Their children were : George Bartlett, Mar. 4, 1825 ; m. Emily Bourne
of Attleboro', Mass., Nov. 30, 1848. He was a Dentist at Orono, Me.,
and Louisville, Ky., and had Twins, George and Willie, Mar. 27,
1854 ; both d. young. Morgan Coleman, Oct. 1866. Albert, Sep. 5,
1826 ; m. and lived in California. Phebe Ann, Jan. 20, 1828 ; ob.
Apr. 17, 1860. Amanda Louisa, Dec. 24, 1830 ; ob. June 23, 1845.
William Dunbar, Jan. 14, 1833 ; m. Georgianna Tritner of Ipswich,
Mass., and settled in Louisville, Ky. Charlotte, Oct. 20, 1835 ; m.
—— Bourne of Attleboro', Mass. Mary Cutler, Dec 2, 1837.
Edwin Franklin, Nov. 8, 1839 ; m. Emma Hotchkiss, Jan. 14, 1866.

58. *Mary*, b. Mar. 18, 1802 ; m. Simeon Newton Cutler of Holliston, Mass., Nov. 8, 1821, and settled in Ashland, Mass., where he d.
Aug. 19, 1867. Issue: Ellen Maria, Nov. 30, 1822 ; m. Joseph Ballard, Nov. 30, 1842, and had Mary Elisabeth, July 5, 1844. George
Edward, Aug. 22, 1824 ; m. Eveline Eames of Holliston, Nov. 4, 1847,
and had Ellen M., Apr. 20. 1851 ; Eva O., Feb. 27, 1853 ; Delia L.,
Jan. 21, 1857 ; ob. May 4, 1857. Henry, July 21, 1825 ; m. Harriet
Dennis, and had Maria L , Aug. 9, 1852; Edwin Herbert, Mar. 6,
1856 ; Grace L., Oct. 9, 1860 ; Henry Willis, Oct. 1, 1865. Delia
Lavina, May 22, 1829 ; m. Joshua Smith, and had Mary L., Oct. 20,
1851 ; ob. June 26, 1853, Martha Jerusha, Aug. 1, 1832 ; m. Benja-
min Thompson of Kennebunk, Me., Feb. 1859, and had Harry O.,
July 25, 1860 ; Samuel C., July 25, 1864 ; ob. July 28, 1866 ; Newton
Cutler, Nov. 9, 1867. Cornelius Howard, m. first Louiza Cook, Sep. 9,
1856, who d. Sep. 1863, and had Adah Frances, Oct. 20, 1858 ; Edward Cornelius, Oct. 10, 1862 ; m. second, Clara Crocker, May, 1864.
William Clark, settled as physician in Chelsea, Mass. ; m. Anna Alden,
May 19, 1862, and had Annie Alden, Mar. 17, 1867. Charles Frederick, m. Lydia Goside, Sep. 24, 1862, and had Jennie Louisa, July 25,
1865.

59. *James Smith*, b. Dec. 31, 1804 ; d. Aug. 23. 1846.

† 60. *David Bucklin*, b. May 10, 1807 ; m. Nov. 15, 1831, ·Nancy
Lathe, b. in Charlton, Mass., Oct. 22, 1812, the dau. of Zephaniah and
Prudence Lathe. He was a clock and watch maker in Holliston and
Boston, and resided at Holliston, Auburndale, and on the homestead at
East Providence. Issue: Mary Louisa, Nov. 14, 1833. Isabella
Bucklin, Nov. 30, 183– ; ob. Apr. 23, 1842. Thomas Bucklin, Feb.
10, 1843. Emma Frances, Nov. 22, 1846 ; ob. Sep. 9, 1847. Charles
Francis, Dec. 10, 1849. Frederick Augustus, June 17, 1852.

61. *Charlotte Delia*, b. Jan. 19, 1811 ; m. Orville Bourne of Lons-
dale, R. I., May 6, 1832, and d. Sep. 18, 1861. Issue : Henry Orville,
Apr. 3, 1832; m. Jennie Case, Sep. 25, 1860, and had Louis Wellington, July 20, 1861 ; ob. Nov. 22, 1866 ; Charlotte Delia, 1864 ; William Clinton, Mar. 7, 1868. Leveneth Bucklin, Mar. 1, 1835 ; ob. May

15, 1835. Charlotte Amelia, May 17, 1836; ob. May 19, 1857. Charles Fitts, Dec. 16, 1837; ob. Apr. 7, 1838. Ann Frances, Oct. 22, 1839; m. Charles Paine of Providence, June 29, 1865. Delia Fitts, Sep. 22, 1843. Ellen Cutler, Dec. 23, 1846. Twins, Stephen Nelson, and Balies Tillotson, Jan. 29, 1850. Walter Eugene, Feb. 23, 1853.

† 62. *Charles Harrison*, b. Apr. 30, 1813; m. Mar. 8, 1839, Emeline Augusta Richards of Dover, who was b. Feb. 1819. He was a carriage maker at East Medway, Mass., where he was Deacon of the Cong. church. Issue: Calvin Richards, Feb. 1840; graduate at Amherst College, 1864; studied at Chicago Seminary; ordained at Medfield, Sep. 5, 1866; installed at Cohasset, June 11, 1868. Julius Augustus, Nov. 1843. Charles Austin, Oct. 1849. Edward Payson, Feb. 1854. Frank Herbert, Apr. 1861.

63. *Abbie Ide*, b. Apr. 30, 1813; m. William Penn Bradley of Stonnington, Ct., Sep. 29, 1844. Issue: William Courtland, Aug. 6, 1845. Abbie Ann, June 23, 1847. Charles Ernest, June 19, 1854. Francis Herbert, May 9, 1859.

† 64. *Joseph Bucklin*, b. Mar. 14, 1818; m. Elizabeth Dennis of Sandwich, Mass., Feb. 22, 1849, and settled on the homestead at Seekonk, now East Providence. Issue: Joseph Dennis, Mar. 16, 1850. David, Apr. 20, 1853. James Sumner, Mar. 12, 1856. Henry Lyman, June 2, 1861.

7

Worcester County Branch.

FOURTH GENERATION.

IV. 5.–14. ROBERT FITTS and HANNAH DIKE, both of Ipswich, were published, " 16, 9, 1717," and married, " Jan. 1, 1717-18, by Rev. Sam¹ Wigglesworth."

They settled in Ipswich, but about 1731 he sold his estate to his brother Abraham, and purchased a farm of Benjamin Marsh in Sutton, where he and his wife united with the Congregational church by letter in 1732. Conveyances of land between him and others took place in 1731, Dec. 7; 1737, Feb. 27, and Oct. 27; 1739, Jan. 27; 1748, Feb. 10, and Feb. 20; 1752, Dec. 22. The mark for his cattle is entered on the Ipswich records as follows: " Robert Fitts' mark of creatures is a hollow crop in yᵉ off ear and half penny in yᵉ same; a crop in yᵉ near ear, a nick in yᵉ under side yᵉ same, and a hole in yᵉ same ear." His Will signed and sealed, May 10, 1753, was presented for Probate, June 15, and allowed, Aug. 22, 1753. It is recorded at Worcester, in volume IV, page 218.

The names of eight children are recorded at Ipswich, and of three others at Sutton :

† 15. *Robert*, b. Nov. 9, 1718; d. 1754; a. 36.
† 16. *Jonathan*, bap. Apr. 24, 1720; d. 1792; a. 75.
  17. *Hannah*, bap. Nov. 19, 1721; d. Dec. 28, 1721.
  18. *Hannah*, bap. Jan. 20, 1723; m. Bartholomew Towne of Sutton, June 27, 1740. They were both admitted to the Congregational church at Sutton, July 26, 1741, and he d. at Sutton in 1783; a. 70 years. Children: Hannah, Apr. 20, 1741; m. Daniel Stone. Bartholomew, Dec. 10, 1742. Abigail, Aug. 3, 1744; m. 1st, Nathan Stone; 2nd, E. Sibley. Reuben, July 29, 1746. Sarah, Apr. 20, 1751. Robert, May 11, 1754. David, Aug. 7, 1756; m. Elizabeth Southworth, Mar. 23, 1780. Mehitable, Sep. 12, 1762. Stephen, Sep. 15, 1765.
  19. *Margarett*, m. —— Little.
† 20. *Benjamin*, bap. Apr. 16, 1728; twice married.
  21. *Mercy*, bap. Mar. 1, 1730.
† 22. *Ebenezer*, bap. Mar. 19, 1732; d. 1790.
  23. *Mehitable* b. Mar. 11, 1733.
  24. *Mary*, b. Oct. 29, 1734.
† 25. *Abraham*, b. Sep. 5, 1739; m. Mary Holman.

FIFTH GENERATION.

V. 14.-15. "ROBERT FITTS, JUᴿ·, of Sutton, and KEZIA TOWNE of Topsfield, were married on yᵉ 9ᵗʰ of November, 1739."

She was born, Feb. 9, 1715, the daughter of William by his second wife Margaret, the widow of John Willard who was executed at Salem during the terrible witchcraft delusion in 1692. The great aunts of Kezia, Rebecca and Mary Towne were also executed, while Sarah barely escaped with her life. Robert Fitts united with the Cong. church in Sutton on profession of his faith in 1741, and died at Sutton in the thirty-sixth year of his age. His Will under date of July 2, 1754, was admitted to Probate, Sep. 9, 1754, and is recorded in volume IV, page 402.

The children were :

26. *Keziah*, b. Jan. 25, 1741 ; m.
† 27. *Robert*, b. Apr. 21, 1742 ; d. Feb. 1826.
† 28. *Samuel*, }
29. *Hannah*, } twins, b. Dec. 12, 1743.
30. *Margarett*, b. Apr. 10, 1745 ; unm.
† 31. *John*, b. June 16, 1747 ; d. May 11, 1836.
32 *Ruth*, b. Apr: 27, 1749 ; unm.
33. *Lucy*, b. Apr. 26, 1751 ; d. young.
34. *Phebe*, b. Aug. 9, 1753.

V. 14.-16. "JONATHAN FITTS and MARY HUTCHINGTON, both of Sutton, were joined in marriage, Novemʳ 27ᵗʰ· 1845, Pʳ the Rev. Mʳ· David Hall, Pastor of the chh. in Sutton."

They lived in Sutton and in Oakham, Mass., whither he moved in 1775. He was chosen Deacon of the church at Oakham, Apr. 11, 1776. He was chosen committee of the church, Nov. 24. 1785, and of the town, Apr. 3, 1786, to confer with Mr. Daniel Tomlinson respecting his settlement in the ministry at Oakham. Deeds of land passed between him and others, 1753, Apr. 23 ; 1754, June 28, and Aug. 5 ; 1756, Feb. 23 ; 1760, Aug. 25 ; 1764, Apr. 8 ; 1767, Apr. 6, and Apr. 8 ; 1770, Nov. 25 ; 1774, Apr. 12 ; 1783, Apr. 4 ; 1789, Mar. 23 ; 1791, May 4. He died in 1792, aged 75, and his wife died, 1806, at the age of 84. His Will dated Oct. 6, 1791, was admitted to Probate, Jan. 1, 1793.

Children all born in Sutton :

35. *Sarah*, b. Sep. 12, 1747 ; m. Benaiah Putnam of Sutton, Dec. 13, 1770.
36. *Tamah*, b. Dec. 15, 1748 ; pub. to Gideon Sibley, Dec. 14, 1771, and m. in Oxford. Apr. 28, 1772.
37. *Mary*, b. Jan. 27, 1750 ; m. Jesse Cummings of Sutton.
38. *Anne*, b. Mar. 10, 1753 ; unm. Her Will with a supplement was dated, Sep. 4, 1806.
39. *Deborah*, b. July 19, 1756 ; m. Benjamin Foster of Oakham, and had issue : Hiram, Deborah, Paul.
40. *Jonathan*, b. May 30, 1758 ; d. young.
41. *Eunice*, b. Mar. 10, 1761 ; d. young.
† 42. *Peter*, b. Sep. 30, 1762 ; d. May 21, 1839 ; a. 76.
43. *Paul*, b. Nov. 31, 1764 ; d. aged 13.

V. 14.-20. " BENJAMIN FITTS and SARAH RICH, both of Sutton, were joined in marriage, Octob^r 31, 1749, P^r the Rev^d M^r· David Hall, Pastor of the first chh. in Sutton." She was a widow at the time of marriage, and her maiden name was Fairfield.

Mr. Fitts had a second wife : " BENJAMIN FITTS and MARY COOK, both of Sutton, were married in Oxford the 19th day of Oct. 1762, by Edward Davis, Justice Peace." She died, Nov. 10, 1837 ; aged 95 years.

The taste of Mr. Fitts in the choice of his wives seems to have changed greatly. His first wife was a widow older than himself with children, his second wife was only twenty when he married her. He resided in Sutton and Oxford where he was a party in the transfer of lands by deed, 1769, Sep. 28 ; 1772, Feb. 22 ; 1776, May 8 ; 1788, May 27. He died at Oxford, Feb. 14, 1803.

The children of Benjamin and Sarah (Rich m. n. Fairfield) Fitts were :

44. *Sarah*, b. Aug. 3, 1750 ; m. —— Griffith.
† 45. *Daniel*, b. Apr. 14, 1758 ; d. 1837 ; a. 84.
† 46. *Walter*, b. Apr. 4, 1755 ; d. Mar. 4, 1825.
† 47. *Robert*, b. Mar 27, 1757 ; d. Dec. 29, 1831.
48. *Edward*, b. Feb. 10, 1759 ; unm.

Children of Benjamin and Mary (Cook) Fitts :

49. *Eunice*, b. Dec. 22, 1763 ; m. Joseph Savery of Sutton. When he went for a marriage certificate he was·asked how he spelled his name, and answered : I–O, Jo ; S–A, Sa ; S–E, Se ;—you know as well as I do Esquire Davis, spell it to suit yourself."

50. *Jonathan*, b. Apr. 3, 1764 ; unm. Tradition says he was killed by the Indians in Ohio.

51. *Mary*, b. Mar. 10, 1765 ; m. David Young ; lived in Jamaica, Vt., and had Jonathan, Job, Willard, Maria, David, (see 151,) and Andrew.

52. *Huldah*, b. June 13, 1766 ; m. Joel Howe of Jamaica, Vt.
† 53. *David*, b. Oct. 3, 1767 ; m. Lucinda Whiting.
† 54. *Benjamin*, b. July 24, 1769 ; d. Sep. 14, 1858.
55. *Mercy*, m. Ezekiel Hovey, and had 15 children.
† 56. *Andrew*, b. Mar. 15, 1773 ; d. July 29, 1849.
· 57. *Hannah*, b. 1780 ; m. Wm. Wiliam and lived in Leicester,
· Mass.

58. *Silas*, b. Feb. 14, 1782 ; unm. He settled in Oxford and either gave or received deeds of land, 1802, Apr. 13 ; 1808, Mar. 14 ; 1810, Apr. 30 ; 1815, Mar. 15, and Sep. 4 ; 1825, Apr. 6 ; 1826, Sep. 30, and Dec· 25.

59. *Mehitable*, m. Asa Savery of Dixfield, Me.
† 60. *Ebenezer*, b. Sep. 16, 1786 ; d. Aug. 18, 1865.
61.—62. Two other children d. in infancy.

V. 14.-22. EBENEZER FITTS married BETHIA HUTCHENSON, and moved from the " eight lots " in Sutton to Dudley, Mass., where he died intestate in 1790. He was a party in the conveyance of land, 1762, Dec. 14 ; 1767, Apr. 4 ; 1771, Nov. 25 ; 1772, Apr. 8 ; 1774, Apr. 1 ; 1783, Mar. 24 ; 1784, Mar. 3 ; 1789, Apr. 7, and Apr. 24 ; 1790, Feb. 20. Commissioners were appointed to set off the widow's thirds, Dec. 7, 1790, and their account was accepted, June 7, 1791. She died at the residence of her son Nathaniel, in Wardsboro', Vt., about the year 1810, near 90 years of age.

Their children were:

† 93. *Caleb*, b. May 25, 1755; d. Feb. 5, 1841.
  64. *Judith*, b. July 30, 1757; pub. to David Lamb of Charlton,. Mass., Jan. 10, 1778.
† 65. *Nathaniel*, b. Aug. 5, 1759; d. Apr. 18, 1837.
† 66. *Ebenezer*, b. Nov. 18, 1761; d. Apr. 7, 1840.
  67. *Lois*, b. Mar. 21, 1771; m. —— Ramsdell, and lived in Wardsboro', Vt.

  V. 14.–25. "ABRAHAM FITTS and MARY HOLMAN, both of Sutton, were joined together in marriage, April 14, 1767, P^r the Rev^d M^r· David Hall, Pastor of ye 1st Chh. in Sutton." He resided in Sutton and Oxford, Mass., and in Dummerston, Vt., giving and receiving deeds of real estate, 1774, July 8; 1777, Feb. and Mar. 1; 1783, Mar. 24; 1784, Apr. 26, and Sep. 21; 1786, Feb. 11; 1788, Feb. 9.

Children, two born in Sutton and two in Oxford:

  68. *Abraham*, b. Nov. 4, 1769.
  69. *Molly*, b. Nov. 25, 1771.
  70. *Sarah*, b. Apr. 27, 1777.
  71. *Anna*, b. Feb. 25, 1787.

SIXTH GENERATION.

  VI. 15.–27. "ROBERT FITTS and LYDIA TOWNE, both of Sutton, were joined together in marriage, June 2, 1767, Pr Benjamin Marsh, Elder of the Baptist chh. in Sutton." She was his cousin; born, Apr. 5, 1739, the daughter of Isaac and Lydia (Estey) Towne.

Second marriage:

ROBERT FITTS and SARAH TREADWELL, (m. n. Nichols) both of Temple-ton, Mass., were married, Apr. 17, 1783, by Rev. Ebenezer Sparkawk. Her first husband was Samuel Treadwell, to whom she was married, June 18, 1766, who died of a cancer on the lip, and by whom she had issue: Samuel, m. Hannah ——. Lydia, Aug. 27, 1768; died Aug. 6, 1836; m. Thomas Larned, who was born, Jan. 10, 1766, and died, July 8, 1834.

Mr. Fitts lived in Sutton, Oxford and Templeton, and died in Tem-pleton, Feb. 1826, his second wife surviving till June, 1829. Deeds of real estate passed between him and others, 1770, Apr. 16; 1772, Jan. 23; 1777, Mar. 21; 1778, Apr. 29; 1793, Nov. 1; 1794, June 5; 1802, Jan. 6; 1805, Jan. 11, and Aug. 17.

The children of Robert and Lydia (Towne) Fitts were:

† 72. *Robert*, m. Kezia Nichols, and d. June 1803.
† 73. *Isaac*, m. Mehitable Bishop.
  74. *Lydia*, relinquished her interest in her mother's thirds, Dec. 29, 1797.

Children of Robert and Sarah (Treadwell, m. n. Nichols) Fitts:

75. *John*, ⎫
76. *Sarah*, ⎬ Twins, b. Dec. 23, 1783, and both died in infancy.

† 77. *George,* b. Jan. 29, 1785 ; d. Nov. 27, 1866.

78. *Sarah,* b. July 2, 1787 ; d. Jan. 31, 1858 ; m. Simeon Gray of Templeton, Feb. 5, 1805, who d. Aug. 1, 1862 ; a. 77, and had issue : Eli, May 29, 1805 ; m. 1st, Lucinda B. Parker ; 2nd, Maria E Hutchinson. George Fitts, Mar. 14, 1807 ; m. Mary B. Wetherell. Elisabeth Treadwell, Jan. 27, 1809. Theodore Courtland, Mar. 16, 1811 ; m. Sally Whitcomb. Sarah Luann, Mar. 6, 1813 ; m. Samuel J. Lyman. Marshall Emerson, Mar. 15, 1816 ; m. Caroline Belknap. Eleanor, July 8, 1818 ; m. Hubbard W. Lawrence. Abigail Nancy, Sep. 21, 1820 ; m. Jonas Phelps. Lucy Rebecca, Sep. 2, 1823 ; d. Sep. 29, 1824. Lucy Rebecca, July 20, 1826 ; m. John Whittemore. Mary, Aug. 24, 1829 ; m. Benjamin E. Thayer.

VI. 15.–28. SAMUEL FITTS and MARTHA STEARNS, were published, Apr. 1, and married, May 14, 1772, by Rev. David Hall of Sutton, Mass. He is supposed to have settled in Vermont.
Their children were :
79. *Clark,* b. Mar. 12, 1773.
80. *Martha,* b. July 11, 1776.
81. *Artemas,* b. Mar 30, 1778.

VI. 15.–31. "JOHN FITTS and REBECKAH STOCKWELL, both of Stuton, were joined together in marriage, Jan^ry 15, 1771, P^r the Rev^d M^r. David Hall, Paster of the 1st Chh. in Sutton." She died at Charlton, Mar. 1, 1774 ; a. 24.

JOHN FITTS and REBECCA DRESSER, were married, Oct. 12, 1775, by Rev. Caleb Curtis, Pastor of the Cong. church in Charlton. She was born, May 6, 1757, and died, Apr. 7, 1841 ; a. 84.

Mr. Fitts was about seven years of age when his father died, and he was put out till he was fourteen for his "vituals and clothes" ; then bound to learn the trade of a carpenter till he was of age. His youthful lot was one of hardship and privation ; he had only one pair of mittens till after he was twenty-one. He was grantor or grantee in deeds of land, 1779, Jan. 15 ; 1783, May 5 ; 1786, Feb. 10 ; 1788, Jan. 1 ; 1792, Apr. 9 ; 1794, May 30 ; 1799, May 3 ; 1802, Mar. 31 ; 1803, Dec. 15 ; 1812, Feb. 12, and Apr. 25 ; 1824, Feb. 26. He died at Charlton, May 11, 1836 ; a. 89.

Children of John and Rebecca (Stockwell) Fitts :
82. *Anna,* b. Oct. 8, 1772 ; d. Nov. 2, 1778.
83. *John,* b. Dec. 16, 1773 ; d. Dec. 22, 1773.
Children of John and Rebecca (Dresser) Fitts :
84. *John,* b. Jan. 6, 1777 ; d. Nov. 6, 1778.
† 85. *Asel,* b. Apr. 10, 1778 ; d. Sep. 10, 1816.
86. *Anna,* b. May 10, 1781 ; unm. She united with the Cong. church in Charlton, Feb. 1811.
† 87. *Roswell,* b. July 7, 1783 ; d. Aug. 14, 1848.
† 88. *John,* b. Oct. 14, 1785, settled on the homestead.
89. *Eunice,* b. Nov. 7, 1788 ; m. John Dunbar, and had Adaline, Dec. 10, 1810. Paskall, May 22. 1812. Aaron D., Nov. 29, 1813. Hannah, d. in infancy. Roderick. Louisa.

90. *Eber*, b. Oct. 16, 1790 ; d. Oct. 21, 1790.

† 91. *Martin*, b. Oct. 11, 1791 ; d. Oct. 15, 1866.

92∗ *Phebe*, b. Oct. 28, 1794 ; m. Calvin Holbrook of Brewer, Me., and had issue: Calista, Nov. 7, 1822. Lorinda, Feb. 13, 1824 ; d. Oct. 27, 1827. John F., Feb. 27, 1825; d. Aug. 7, 1828. Louisa, Oct. 17, 1826 ; d. Oct. 17, 1827. Lucy, Sep. 9, 1828; d. Mar. 17, 1834. Julia Ann, July 21, 1830 ; d. Mar. 7, 1834. Chester, May 25, 1832. Fannie Elvira, Nov. 16, 1834. John Chandler, June 16, 1837. Elvira, Aug. 23, 1839 , d. Nov. 5, 1844.

93. *Lury*, b. Dec. 12, 1797; pub. to Charles Chickering of Dedham, Aug. 7, 1825. They settled in Pawtucket, R. I., and he d. Aug. 26, 1841. Children: Ann, Sep. 19, 1826. Charles E., June 14, 1828. Rebecca L., Jan. 5, 1830 ; d. Dec. 28, 1835.

94. *Rebecca*, b. May 22, 1802 ; pub. Dec. 25, 1825, to Eben. Cook Mann of Cavendish, Vt., and m. by Rev. James Boomer. They settled in Proctorsville, Ct., from which place in 1833, she brought a letter to the Cong. church in Charlton. Children : Francis F., Dec. 13, 1826 ; m. in New York city, Adaline Taylor, Feb. 2, 1829. Philura M., June 25, 1828 ; d. Feb. 2, 1829. Chester Q., Nov. 25, 1830 ; d. Mar. 1833.

VI. 16.–42. PETER FITTS of Oakham, married first, LYDIA PERRY of Oakham, who died, 1810 ; a. 49 ; and second, in 1811, LUCY KNIGHT, (m. n. Howe) of Athol.

He was a party in the transfer of lands by deeds, 1804, Nov. 9 ; 1805, Nov. 7, and Nov. 13, and Nov. 30 ; 1810, May 26 ; 1815, Mar. 2 ; 1817, Mar. 28 ; 1825, Feb. 10 ; 1827, Mar. 6 ; 1831, Jan. 29. He was for many years an exemplary member of the Cong. church in Oakham, and died, May 21, 1839 ; a. 76. His Will dated, May 18, 1839, was approved the first Tuesday of July, 1839, and is recorded in volumn LXXXIV, page 16.

The children by his first wife were:

95. *Jonathan*, b. Sep. 7, 1790 ; d. Nov. 27, 1807.

† 96. *Jesse*, b. Mar. 24, 1792 ; d. May 22, 1853.

97. *Zadock*, b. Mar. 28, 1794 ; d. in infancy.

98. *Mary*, b. June 3, 1796 ; m. Frederick A. Presho of Oakham, Jan. 22, 1817. This aged couple celebrated their golden wedding, Jan. 22, 1867, when their hearts were made glad by the substantial gifts, and the good will and respect of many friends and visitors.

† 99. *Elisha*, b. Mar. 29, 1799 ; d. May 3, 1836.

VI. 20.–45. " DANIEL FITTS and CHLOE WHITE, both of Sutton, were joined together in marriage, April 9, 1778, Pᵣ Jeremiah Barstow, Pastor of the first Baptist Chh. in Sutton." They settled in Oxford, where he was grantor or grantee of land by deed, 1789, Mar. 23 ; 1794, Nov. 7 ; 1796, Apr. 2 ; 1798, Mar. 12 ; 1812, Feb. 22 ; 1815, Apr. 16 ; 1821, Apr. 2 ; 1831, July 5; 1832, Jan. 9. They both died in Oxford, 1837 ; she, Jan. 22 ; a. 80, and he, Feb. 13 ; a. 84. His Will was dated, Apr. 9, 1823, and presented for Probate, Apr. 4, 1837.

Their children were:

100. *Sally*, b. Dec. 18, 1779; second wife of Abijah Lamb of Oxford.

101. *Chloe*, b. Apr. 19, 1781; m. William Henderson of Vt.

102. *Sophia*, b. Nov. 10, 1783; second wife of Reuben Adams of Auburn, whose first wife was Mary Fitts (124).

† 103. *Daniel*, b. Jan. 6, 1785; m. Lydia Livermore.

104. *Caroline*, b. Aug. 4, 1786; m. Joshua Burrill of Tompson, Ct. He was a hotel keeper in Onondaga Co., and in Righville, Genesee Co., N. Y., and his children were: Patty, m. —— Redman, and had 12 children. Acksah, m. John King, and had 4 children. Arba, m. and had a family. Mahaleth, m. and had no children.

105. *Abijah*, b. Sep. 7, 1788; d. young.

106. *Roxilana*, b. June 23, 1792; m. John Burrill, a brother of Joshua, and a descendant of Lord Burrill of King's Deer Park of Wales, Eng.

† 107. *John*, b. June 13, 1794; twice married.

† 108. *Arba*, b. Sep. 14, 1796; d. Mar. 24, 1856.

109. *Tirza*, b. Nov. 11, 1800; d. young.

VI. 20.–46. "The intentions of marriage between WALTER FITTS of Oxford, and SARAH MERIAM of the County Gore, were entered, June the 10th, 1778, and published in Oxford as the law directs, Per Samuel Harris, town clerk." She was the daughter of Ebenezer and Elisabeth (Locke) Meriam, and born at the "County Gore" in Oxford, Feb. 3, 1760. She was the grand daughter of Ebenezer and Elisabeth (Meriam) Locke of Lexington, who was impressed before 1746, probably in the French War. Her great grandfather was Dea. William Locke, householder, selectman, &c., in Woburn, 1703–4, and 1732, whose father Dea. William was born at Stepney Parish, London, Eng., Dec. 13, 1628.

Mr. Fitts resided at Oxford, Warwick, Auburn and Charlton; had a second wife, the WIDOW BLANCHARD, and died, Mar. 4, 1825; a. 70.

The children of Sarah (Meriam) Fitts were:

110. *Miriam*, b. Feb. 14, 1779; m. Nathan Pratt of Charlton and Sturbridge, June 29, 1795, by Rev. Elias Dwelly.

111. *Betsey*, b. Nov, 5, 1780; m. James Cudworth of Auburn, 1801, had 8 children and d. July, 1821.

† 112. *Walter*, b. Jan. 12, 1783; m. Mary Cozens.

113. *Sylvanus*, b. Mar. 22, 1785; d. Nov. 20, 1785.

114. *Sarah*, b. Sep. 15, 1787 or '8; m. Israel, son of Absalom Stockwell of Worcester, 1819, and had three children.

† 115. *Jonathan*, b. Aug. 13, 1791; m. Laminda Hobbs.

116. *Martha*, b. June 9, 1793 or '4; pub. Apr. 4, 1817, to Stephen Gould Livermore, son of Reuben of Sudbury; had 10 children, and d. at Millbury, Sep. 18, 1844.

117. *Celia*, b. Dec. 17, 1796; d. at Auburn, Sep. 1802.

118. *Jotham*, b. Sep. 14, 1799; d. at Auburn, Sep. 1802.

119. *Celia*, b. Dec. 24, 1802; m. her cousin Jeremiah Pratt, Jun. 20, 1821; had 10 children, and d. at Greenfield, Mass., Apr. 13, 1849.

VI. 20.–47. "The intentions of marriage between ROBERT FITTS, JUN[r,] and PHEBE PATCH, both of Oxford, were entered, August the 8th, 1778, and published in Oxford as the law directs, per Samuel Harris, Town Clerk." They were married, Aug. 25, 1778, by the Rev. Joseph Bowman.

Mr. Fitts resided in Oxford, Warwick, Sutton, Charlton and Auburn. When a boy he lived with his uncle Abraham. The uncle being drafted in the time of the Revolution, Robert, then sixteen, went as his substitute and served several months in the army. While in the service he was offered a lieutenant's commission, which however, he de-declined, preferring the quiet of civil life. He was married when but little over twenty-one, and with only one suit of clothes to his back; yet he brought up a large family and became worth his thousands. He was grantor or grantee in the transfer of real estate by deeds, 1780, Oct. 13; 1781, Nov. 12; 1786, June 24; 1790, Feb. 3; 1791, Mar. 15; 1792, Oct. 8, Nov. 21, and Nov. 22; 1793, Aug. 1; 1796, Jan. 15; 1798, Mar. 11; 1802, Mar. 16, and Dec. 20; 1803, Jan. 13, and Feb. 10; 1806, Dec. 3; 1808, Mar. 2, Mar. 4, and Mar. 11; 1809, Sep. 20; 1810, Feb. 21; 1811, Mar. 30, Mar. 27, and Apr. 24; 1812, Mar. 7; 1814, Apr. 27, and May 31; 1822, Oct. 28; 1823, Jan. 22; 1825, Jan. 31; 1826, Mar. 22, and May 13; 1827, Oct. 30; 1830, Jan. 8, and Oct. 7. He spent the last of his days in Auburn where he was highly respected in church and community. His Will dated Mar. 14, 1827, was presented for Probate, Mar. 6, 1832, and is recorded at Worcester, volume LXXII, page 307. He died Dec. 29, 1831; aged 74.

> " The sweet remembrance of the just
> Shall flourish when they sleep in dust."
>
> *Tombstone.*

The children were :

120. *Rhoda*, b. Sunday, May 30, 1779; m. first, Roger Bartlett of Charlton; second, Nathan Haskell of Wendall, and lived in Leverett and Wendall. She d. Sunday, Jan. 17, 1830; a. 50. No children.

† 121. *Edward*, b. Monday, Mar. 26, 1781; d. Sep. 19, 1854.

† 122. *Rufus*, b. Monday, Jan. 16, 1786; m. Lucy Sanderson.

123. *Anna*, b. Saturday, Mar. 15, 1788; m. Porter Nutting of Leverett, Jan. 22, 1809. She had several children, and d. Apr. 7, 1839; a. 51.

124. *Polly*, b. Tuesday, Apr. 20, 1790; m. Reuben Adams, lived in Charlton, and d. Sunday, June 7, 1812; a. 22. No children. Mr. Adams afterward m. Sophia Fitts (102).

† 125. *Robert*, b. Tuesday, Aug. 5, 1794; m. Lucy Bangs.

126. *Phebe*, b. Thursday, Aug. 5, 1797; pub. to Alden Wood of Leverett, Nov. 1817, and m. by Rev. Enoch Pond, D. D., Jan. 15, 1818. Several children.

† 127. *Hervey*, b. Friday, Nov. 22, 1799; twice married.

128. *James*, b. Monday, July 30, 1804; m. Sally Ball of Leverett, by whom he had children: Orus, Martha, Emeline, Gertrude, Sarah, Rufus. He was also m. a second time.

VI. 20.–53. "The intentions of marriage between DAVID FITTS of Oxford, and LUCINDA WHITING of Plainfield, were entered, Feb. 2nd,

1795, and published in Oxford as the law directs, per Samuel Harris, Town Clerk." He resided at Oxford and Charlton, Mass., and died at Providence, R. I. Deeds of lands to which he was a party are recorded at Worcester under under the dates of 1812, June 6 ; 1813, Oct. 29 ; 1816, July 23 ; 1817, Feb. 27.

The children were:

† 129. *Abijah Whiting*, b. Nov. 6, 1795 ; m. Elisabeth Penrow.
130. *Lucinda*, b. June 6, 1800 ; d. young.
131. *Levi*, b. Sep. 1, 1802 ; d. aged about 20.
132. *David*, b. Sep. 11, 1804.
133. *Palmer*, b. Sep. 7, 1806 ; d. young.
.134. *Harriot*, b. Apr. 24, 1809 ; m. William Hudson of Providence, and had several children.

VI. 20.–54. "BENJAMIN FITTS, JUNR., and SARAH RICH, both of Charlton, were married by Ebenezer Learned, Esqr., September 28th. 1794." She was the daughter of Benjamin and Rebecca (Daggett) Rich, and died Sep. 2, 1845 ; a. 75. It is quite a remarkable coincidence that two individuals, father and son, by the same name, should marry two other persons also bearing the same name. (See 20.) He either gave or received deeds of land in Oxford where he resided, 1799, Mar. 11 ; 1801, Feb. 10 ; 1806, Apr. 29 ; 1808, Mar. 14 ; 1812, Apr. 13 ; 1814, Mar. 26 ; 1815, Sep. 4 ; 1816, Feb. 6 ; 1817, Feb. 1, and Feb. 11 ; 1821, Jan. 22, and Mar. 4. He died Sep. 14, 1868 ; a. 89.

The children were:

135. *Cynthia*, b. 1795 ; d. aged 3 years.
136. *Samuel*, b. June 10, 1797 ; unm. ; d. Sep. 3, 1844 ; a. 47.
† 137. *Clark*, b. Oct. 7, 1799 ; m. Hannah R. Putnam.
† 138. *Alvin*, b. Aug. 29, 1801 ; m. Lucy Stevens.
† 139. *David*, b. Dec. 5, 1805 ; m. Chloe Nichols.
† 140. *Lewis*, b. Dec. 10, 1807 ; d. 1853 ; a. 46.

VI. 20.–56. ANDREW FITTS of Oxford, married first, RUTH PIKE. She was the daughter of George and Mary (Seaver) Pike, and born Aug. 24, 1793, and died Apr. 27, 1833 ; a. 40. He married second, ELEANOR PIKE, a sister of his first wife, April, 1835. He was a party in the transfer of lands by deed in Oxford and Charlton, 1796, Mar. 16 ; 1805, May 9 ; 1808, Mar. 14 ; 1813, 1814, Mar. 22 ; 1819, Jan. 27 ; 1802, Sep. 11 ; 1821, Jan. 5 ; 1827, May 15 ; 1829, Sep. 5. He died July 29, 1849 ; a. 76. Thirds set off to Eleanor Fitts, his widow, May 7, 1850.

The children were all by the first marriage :

† 141. *Harrison*, b. Mar. 13, 1815 ; m. Nancy Houston.
142. *Fannie*, b. May 6, 1816 ; m. May 21, 1851, by Rev. Daniel E. Chapin of the Meth. Epis. church, Martin Aldrich of Webster who was the son of Jesse and Susanna (Keith) Aldrich. Their children were: Frances Ida, July 23, 1853. Lydia Ines, Nov. 6, 1855.
† 143. *Benjamin*, b. May 30, 1817 ; m. Aurelia Pristol.
144. *George Pike*, b. Sep. 25, 1818 ; d. June 9, 1855.
† 145. *Sumner*, b. Jan. 4, 1820 ; twice married.
146. *Emeline*, b. Aug. 27, 1821.

147. *Lydia Ann*, b. May 28, 1823 ; m. Jeremiah C. Sholes of Sturbridge, May 18, 1845, and d. Oct. 9, 1851, leaving Erwin J., Jan. 2, 1848. Frank —— July 3, 1851.

148. *Elisabeth*, b. Dec, 9, 1824 ; m. William C. Hart of Pomfret, Vt., Aug. 16, 1847 ; lived in Cornish, N. H., and had issue : George A., July, 1848. Wm. Lazell, June, 1850. Ella Elisabeth, Mar. 1853. Willis, Apr. 1856. Etta, June, 1867.

149. *Mary Louisa*, b. Sep. 30, 1827 ; d. Sep. 14, 1846.

> " Farwell sister ! angels bear thee
> On their wings to courts above ;
> Kindred spirits there shall greet thee,
> While they join in strains of love."

† 150. *Andrew Nelson*, b. Mar. 9, 1829.

VI. 20.-60. EBENEZER FITTS married ELIZA COBURN, and settled in Oxford, where he received deeds of land, 1826, May 6, and Sep. 30 ; 1829, Apr. 1 ; and died, Aug. 18, 1865.

Their children were :

151. *Adaline*, b. Feb. 3, 1809 ; m. David Young, son of David and Mary (Fitts) Young, (51), of Jamaica, Vt. They settled in Oxford, Mass., and had issue : An infant son, d. 1835. Artemas, Feb. 20, 1837. Mary Eliza, Jan. 22, 1839.

† 152. *Silas*, b. 1811 ; m. Lucetta B. Larcom.

153. *Palmer*, b. Sep. 3, 1813. When about 23 he mysteriously disappeared and no trace of him was ever discovered.

† 154. *Linus*, b. Dec. 31, 1817 ; m. Laura Ann Hodges.

155. *Mary E.*, b. Aug. 27, 1820 ; m. Wm. A. Ellis of Oxford, had issue : Ella Augusta, and Linus, and d. Mar. 16, 1867.

† 156. *Levi*, b. Aug. 7, 1826 ; m. Prudence Balcom.

VI. 22.-69. " Marriage intended between CALEB FITTS of Dudley, and RACHEL PATCH of Oxford, July y* 18th, 1780." They were married, Aug. 1, 1780, and settled in Charlton, where she died, Nov. 14, 1831 ; a. 68 ; having been born, July 27, 1763, the daughter of Andrew, and the sister of Phebe Patch, who married Robert Fitts, (47.)

Caleb Fitts was baptized and with his wife admitted to communion with the Cong. church in Charlton under the pastoral care of Rev. Erastus Larned, Sep. 14, 1800. He was a party to the transfer of lands by deed, 1782, Dec. 10 ; 1787, Oct. 8 ; 1791, June 24 ; 1792, Mar. 19 ; 1797, Mar. 10 ; 1802, Oct. 26 ; 1805, Dec. 16 ; 1806, June 24 ; 1815, Sep. 8 ; 1816, May 13, and Aug. 6 ; 1819, July 12 ; 1824, Nov. 30. He died, Feb. 5, 1841.

The children were :

157. *Andrew P.*, b. July 12, 1781 ; d. Nov. 16, 1789.

† 158. *Charles*, b. Dec. 19, 1783 ; bap. Sep. 14, 1800.

159. *Mary*, b. June 6, 1786 ; bap. Sep. 14, 1800 ; m. Rufus Twiss; had issue : William ; Hannah ; Clarissa, b. June 16, 1813, and d. Aug. 10, 1816.

160. *Rachel*, b. Apr. 3, 1789 ; d. May 16, 1789.

161. *Rachel*, b. Nov. 8, 1790 ; bap. Sep. 14, 1800 ; m. Nathaniel Heyward, Mar. 1820, and lived in Rochester, N. Y.

162.　*Clarissa,* b. Oct. 7, 1792 ; bap. Sep. 14, 1800'; d. June 16, 1813.

163.　*Chloe,* b. Mar. 21, 1796 ; bap. Sep. 14, 1800, and admitted to full communion with the Cong. church in Charlton, Aug. 22, 1824 ; m. Samuel Mayo of Oxford, Feb. 1825, and d. 1864.

† 164.　*Caleb,* b. Jan. 7, 1799 ; bap. Sep. 14, 1800.

165. · *Lucina,* b. Oct. 19, 1801 ; bap. Sep. 12, 1802 ; m. David Dodge of Oxford, Aug. 1825, and d. Aug. 11, 1824.

† 166.　*Andrew Patch,* b. Mar. 24, 1804 ; bap. July 29, 1804, by Rev. Edward Whipple.

167.　*Leonard,* b. Dec. 21, 1807 ; d. Oct. 11, 1810.

VI.　22.–65.　Nathaniel Fitts married Sarah Ramsdell of Wardsboro', Vt., in 1793. About 1790 he moved from Dudley, Mass., to Wardsboro', Vt., where he settled on a farm and died, June 13, 1849 ; a. 90. She died, Apr. 18, 1837 ; a. 72.

Their children were :

† 168.　*Levi,* b. Jan. 10, 1795 ; m. Artene Clark.

169.　*Nathaniel,* b. Mar. 25, 1797 ; d. June 1808.

† 170.　*Amasa,* b. July 23, 1800 ; m. Eliza Ward.

† 171.　*Ebenezer,* b. Nov. 2, 1802 ; d. July 19, 1847.

172.　*Sarah,* b. Feb. 3, 1805 ; m. Joseph E. Knowlton, and lived in Wardsboro' and Jamaica, Vt., and had issue : Adaline S., Nov. 15, 1824. Emory J., Mar. 12, 1826 ; m. Adaline Pierce. Gilbert N., Sep. 16, 1828 ; d. Dec. 15, 1847. William F., Nov. 7, 1831 ; m. Ellen Bingham. Orin F., Feb. 14, 1835 ; m. C. F. Haskell. Laura A., Mar. 30, 1838 ; m. William H. Carr. Julia H., Aug. 30, 1840 ; m. Charles S. Clark. Edwin, Mar. 13, 1844 ; d. Aug. 11, 1844.

173.　*Joanna,* b. Aug. 28, 1808 ; m. Abner White, May 30, 1855, and d. at Wardsboro', May 15, 1864, leaving no children.

174.　*Laura,* b. June 11, 1811 ; m. Willard Johnson, lived in Dover and South Wardsboro' and had Norman C., Apr. 8. 1836. Arosette A., Sep. 5, 1846.

VI.　22.–66.　"Ebenezer Fitts, Jun²·' and Mary Mansfield, both of Dudley, were married, Decem^r 15th, 1785, by Charles Gleason, Clerk." She was born, Feb. 12, 1766. His name occurs in conveyances of real estate, 1786, Mar. 20 ; 1790, Apr. 7 ; 1810, Jan. 7, and Jan. 8 ; 1811, Dec. 3 ; 1817, Aug. 4 ; 1820, Apr. 20. He died, Apr. 7, 1840.

"MRS. MARY FITTS,
wife of
MR. EBENEZER FITTS,
died
March 13, 1826,
Æ. 60.
After a long and distressing sickness which she bore with patience
and a resignation and a full
faith of an immortality."

Tombstone in Dudley.

Their children were:
175. *Samuel*, b. Oct. 6, 1786 ; pub. to Eunice, dau. of Thomas Case, Esq., Oct. 26, 1812. They lived in Charlton, where he took deeds of land, 1829, Jan. 17 ; 1830, June 28. No children.
176. *Polly* b. Jan. 26, 1789 ; m. May 28, 1805, Reuben Albee, who was b. Apr. 8, 1784. Issue: Emily, Nov. 14, 1806 ; d. Nov. 19, 1819. Serina, Aug. 14, 1808 ; d Nov. 3, 1836. Cyrus, Aug. 2, 1811 ; unm. Alford, Oct. 20, 1815 ; a physician in Pascove, R. I. ; d. Oct. 22, 1850. Reuben.
177. *Sally*, b. May 1, 1797 ; m. Caleb Pope, lived in Dudley and Oxford, and had Effingham, d. young. Emily, m. Lyman Laws.
178. *Leafy*, b. July 9, 1802 ; m. Dexter Alden of Southboro' ; pub. Feb. 12, 1820, lived in Webster, and had a dau., d. in infancy ; Samuel; George; Loritta.

SEVENTH GENERATION.

VII. 27.–72. " The intentions of marriage between M^r· ROBERT FITTS and M^rs· KEZIA NICHOLS have been entr^d and published as the law directs—Royalston, Ap^r· 6th, A. D. 1793." They were married, Apr. 21, 1793, by Rev. Joseph Lee, and settled in Royalston, Mass., where he died, June, 1803. Inventory of his estate returned, Aug. 10, 1803.
Their children were :
† 179. *Robert*, b. Oct. 19, 1793 ; m. Tryphena Farrar, June 5, 1821, who d. Oct 17, 18♠2. Issue: Robert, Mar. 26, 1822 ; m. first, Marie L. Wood, Sep. 1, 1843, who d. Mar. 9, 1850, by whom he had Georgia L., Bella T., R. Almonte, and Samuel A. Second, m. Marie T. Buck, Sep. 1853, by whom he had Willie E., and Lauretta M. Mary T.; Feb. 10, 1824 ; m. John M. White, 1847, and had M. Frement, M. Josephine, and Ida H. Kezia A., June 27, 1826 ; m. Thomas C. Kenyon, 1857, and had Ellen T., and Jeannie F. Samuel L., July 23, 1830 ; m. N. Jeannie Sheppard, 1854. Lucy A., June 30, 1833. George W., Nov. 24, 1836 ; d. Mar. 20, 1837. Honora, Dec. 9, 1839 ; d. Sep. 28, 1840.
180. *A daughter*, d. Sep. 2, 1798 ; a. 2 years.
181. *A son*, d. Nov. 13, 1800 ; a. 4 months.
182. *George*, b. Apr. 20, 1803 ; d. Sep. 18, 1804.

VII. 27.–73. ISAAC FITTS married MEHITABLE BISHOP, and lived in Sutton and Royalston, Mass , and Fitzwilliam, N. H. Deeds of land to which he was a party are recorded at Worcester under the following dates, 1792, Apr. 8 ; 1793, Jan. 30, and Apr. 4 ; 1797, Aug. 15, and Dec. 25 ; 1799, Apr. 15, and Sep. 16 ; 1801, Apr. 23, Oct. 26, and Dec. 10.
Their children were :
183. *Lydia*, b. July 13, 1795 ; m. Jedediah Allen of Holden, and had Lucy, m. —— Burkley, and Calvin.
184. *Isaac*, b. Dec. 20, 1796 ; m. Prudence Dunster of Gardner, and settled in Rochester, N. Y. A mason by trade.

185. *Lucy B.*, b. July 29, 1798 ; unm.
186. *Melinda*, b. June 11, 1800 ; d. Aug. 17, 1802.
187. *Pharinda B.*, b. Mar. 4, 1802 ; m. Elisha Bailey, and d. soon after.
† 188. *Luke G.*, b. Feb. 20, 1804 ; m. Lydia Drake, 1827. She was the dau. of Bezer Drake of Pembroke, and d. Nov. 10, 1863. Children : (1) A daughter, 1828 ; m. Charles Leavitt, and had Charles Melvin, Edwin Thomas, Julia, Susan, Lydia, William, Henry, Urana, Robert. (2) Isaac Newton, m. widow Mary (Tucker) Gardner. (3) Luke G., m. Paulina Langdon, and had five children. He lost a hand in the army and drew a pension. (4) Welcome W., m. Mary A., dau. of Wm. and Hannah O. (Howland) Daniels, and had Randal Bartlett, who d. an infant. He d. previous to 1866, and his widow m. George Thayer, Feb. 3, 1866. (5) John, d. in his fourth year. (6) Lyman Bezer. (7) Seth Otis, m. Abbie Gardner.
189. *Phebe*, b. Dec. 3, 1805 ; also m. Elisha Bailey, and had several children.
190. *Phyletha F.*, b. Jan. 13, 1808 ; m. Wm. Johnson of Templeton, and had Cereta.
191. *Lucina W.*, b. Nov. 2, 1810 ; m. John Lewis of Townsend, and had John and Lucina.
192. *Lyman*, b. Jan. 5, 1812, at Winchendon.
193. *John*, b. July 11, 1814 ; m. Maria Hale, and had children.
194. *Tryphrey*, b. Dec. 18, 1816, at Fitzwilliam.
195. *Emeline*, m. Nathan Sylvester of Townsend, and had children.
196. *Angelina Rebecca*, m. Wm. Withington of Winchester, and had children. He was the son of Wm. the son of Elisha, who was b. at Stowe, Mar. 21, 1746.

———

VII. 27.-77. GEORGE FITTS married first, SALLY HOLMES, June 27, 1809, by Rev. Charles Wellington, and second, NANCY CROSBY, Jan. 5, 1815. He lived in Templeton, Athol and Barre, Mass., and in Bangor, Me., where he died, Nov. 27, 1866. He was a cabinet maker, and goldsmith. He was a party to the transfer of real estate by deeds recorded at Worcester, 1808, Apr. 6, and June 28 ; 1809, Oct. 11 ; 1813, Feb. 20, Apr. 1, and Aug. 2 ; 1815, May 20 ; 1816, Jan. 24 ; 1823, May 12.
The children of George and Sally (Holmes) Fitts were :
197. *Caroline*, b. June 23, 1810 ; m. Marshall W. Atwood of Barre, Jan. 1835, and had George Marshall, Mar. 26, 1836 ; d. Mar. 3, 1856. She afterward m. Jesse Belknap, Sep. 20, 1842, and had Albert W., Sep. 19, 1843.
198. *Sally Luann*, b. July 21, and d. Dec. 27, 1812.
The children of George and Nancy (Crosby) Fitts were :
199. *Sarah Luann*, b. Nov. 27, 1815 ; m. Edward W. Bartlett, Oct. 2, 1845, and had Edward W., Feb. 29, 1847. She d. Sep. 21, 1858.
200. *Marietta Williams*, b. May 3, 1821 ; m. William Arnold, Jan. 25, 1840, and had Wm. O., Jan. 4, 1842. Eva, Mar. 9, 1846. Maud, Jan. 7, 1860.
201. *George Coelebs*, b. Mar. 21, 1823 ; d. Nov. 9, 1850.

VII. 31.–85. "Mr. Asahel Fitts and Miss Anna Clemens, both of Charlton, were married, Jany 19th, 1802, by E. Larned." She was born, Mar. 1781, and died, July 8, 1818. He lived in Charlton, where he died intestate, Sep. 10, 1816; a. 38.

Their children were :

† 202. *Ashel Eliott*, b. June 24, 1802 ; m. Lois Emerson, settled in Southbridge, and had Ashel, Mary Ann, A daughter, Paschal, Henry, who d. a major in the army.

† 203. *Francis*, b. Mar. 10, 1804 ; m. Eliza Dean of West Woodstock, Ct., Nov. 1, 1835. She was b. Jan. 11, 1811. He was a merchant in Michigan and in Chicago, Ill. Issue : Edward, Oct. 26, 1836; d. Mar. 22, 1837. Ellen, July 3, 1838. May Elizabeth, Aug. 30, 1840. Lucy Ann, May 26, 1843 ; d. Feb. 26, 1845. Eliza, Feb. 26, 1845 ; d. Feb. 1, 1855. Joseph Edwin, Mar. 3, 1850. Francis Dean, Mar. 14, 1854.

† 204. *Paschal*, b. July 8, 1806 ; m. first, Apr. 5, 1831, Eliza King of Charlton, who was b. Aug. 9, 1804, and d. Feb. 11; 1863 ; m. second, Mar. 29, 1864, Maria L. Noyes, who was b. at Plainfield, Ct., Sep. 6, 1815. He lived in Groton, N. Y., and had by first marriage, (1) John, Dec. 12, 1632 ; d. Dec. 26, 1832. (2) George, Mar. 2, 1836 ; m. Nov. 16, 1858, Semantha D. Colvert, who was b. Sep. 1839, and had Jerome Colvert, Feb. 12, 1860 ; Fred, May 31, 1862. (3) Lucy Ann, Sept. 1; 1837.

205. *John*, b, Nov. 5, 1807 ; d. Aug. 15, 1810.

† 206. *Roswell*, b. Apr. 20, 1809 ; m. Almira Clark, Oct. 10, 1833, who was b. Jan. 12, 1809, and resided in Leroy and Cuyahoga Falls, Ohio. Issue : Otis, June 23, 1834. Ann Maria, Apr. 8, 1836 ; m. Lyman K. Cox. Mary Jane, Dec. 16, 1837 ; m. Ephraim H. Freeman. Francis, Mar. 19, 1840 ; d. June 6, 1841. Dexter W., Feb. 2, 1844. George P., Dec. 2, 1846. Eliza C., Feb. 16, 1848. Lucy A., Apr. 20, 1850.

207. *Ann Maria*, b. Jan. 1, 1811 ; m. July 14, 1835, John Boynton, who was b. July 2, 1798, and settled in Groton, N. Y.

208. *Caroline*, b. July 11, 1813 ; m. Oct. 25, 1831, Aaron Woodbury, who was b. Aug. 1, 1807, and lived at Groton, N. Y.

209. *Bradford*, b. Jan. 15, 1815 ; d. Feb. 13, 1815.

210. *Philip*, b. Nov. 11, 1816 ; d. Jan. 10, 1817.

VII. 31.–87. Roswell Fitts married Elisabeth Ward, Nov. 25, 1808, who was born June 21, 1785, the daughter of Elijah and Rachel (Nichols) Ward of Charlton, Mass., and died in Dedham; Me., Sep. 27, 1839. They lived in Oxford, Mass., and in Eddington and Dedham, Me. He died at Holden, Me., Aug. 14, 1848.

The children were :

† 211. *Elijah T.*, b. Aug. 23, 1809 ; m. Emeline E. Gilmore of Wrentham, Mass., Nov. 6, 1834, who was b. Jan. 19, 1816. They moved to Santa Clara, Cal., in 1854. Issue : William Francis, Oct. 5, 1836 ; m. Delorus Pinedo, Mar. 31, 1864, and had Wm. Lewis, Emeline Delorus. Salem Grant, June 30, 1843 ; d. Aug. 23, 1845. Lucy Jane, Aug. 23, 1847. Miranda Lois, Jan. 23, 1850 ; d. Oct. 15, 1850. Ada Busford, Dec. 16, 1856.

212. *Eliza,* b. Apr. 1, 1812 ; m. Putnam Wilson of Holden, and had issue : Adelaide E., Mar. 7, 1841. Josephine A., June 14, 1844. Jerusha D., June 8, 1847. Marshall P., Feb. 24, 1850 ; d. Sep. 29, 1854.

† 213 *Aaron,* b. July 18, 1814 ; m. Elisabeth F. Wheeler, Oct. 26, 1843, and settled in Dedham, Me. Issue : Emma, Aug. 19, 1844. George W., Feb. 24, 1846. Ellis M., June 16, 1857. Angelia L., Jan. 28, 1859. Roswell F., Oct. 2, 1860.

214. *Frances,* b. June 29, 1816 ; m. George W. Thompson of Bangor, Me., July 10, 1845, and had Frances J., June 5, 1846. George A., June 13, 1849.

215. *Parmelia,* b. Dec. 5, 1818 ; m. Charles Leighton of Brewer, Me., Sep. 10, 1848, and had Maria E., May 18, 1850. Parmelia F., June 12, 1854.

216. *Phœbe,* b. July 20, 1821 ; m. Thomas R. Copeland of Brewer, Me., July 15, 1841. Issue : Roswell F., Nov. 7, 1643. Lemuel C., Nov. 25. 1845. Salem D., Mar. 29, 1848. Herbert L., Aug. 7, 1852 ; d. Nov. 29, 1853. Thomas F., Apr. 2, 1856 ; d. July 30, 1857. Lilian A., Apr. 23, 1858. Albra S., Feb. 8, 1861. Willie H., Nov. 7, 1863.

217. *Francis,* b. Nov. 2, 1823 ; d. Aug. 23, 1826.

218. *Lury,* b. May 9, 1826 ; m. James Emery of Berwick, Me., Sep. 7, 1852, and had Alicia T., Oct. 27, 1853. Martha A., Feb. 18, 1859.

219. *Elisabeth,* b. Feb. 18, 1830 ; m. Sep. 8, 1851, Rev. Edw. P. Kimball, grad. Bangor Theological Seminary, 1850, settled in Clinton, Mass., and in Monticello, Iowa. They had children.

VII. 31.–88. COL. JOHN FITTS of Charlton, Mass., was published to LUCY MOORE TOWN, Aug. 12, 1810, and married by Rev. Edward Whipple, pastor of the Cong. church in Charlton. After her death, June 11, 1811, at the age of 23 years, he married CATHERINE TOWN, published, May 3, 1813, who died, Apr. 3, 1849 ; a. 56.

Issue by first marriage :

220. *Lucy Moore Town,* b. Jan. 27, 1811 ; m. Dr. Charles M. Fay of Charlton, Jan. 1829, and d. Feb. 5, 1839.

Issue by second marriage :

† 221. *Lewis L.,* b. Dec. 5, 1813 ; m. Emily Ward, Apr. 10, 1842, and settled in Springfield, Mass. She was b. Dec. 24, 1816, the dau. of Simon and Martha (Blood) Ward of Charlton. Children : Edwin A., Mar. 4, 1843 ; d. Sep. 19, 1843. Louisa Town, Feb. 15, 1845. Edward L., May 18, 1847 ; d. Aug. 28, 1850. Ann Rebecca, Aug. 20, 1849 ; d. Sep. 4, 1850. Kate Isabella, Oct. 29, 1851 ; d. May 19, 1865; Alice Malvina, Oct. 22, 1853 ; d. Apr. 4, 1854. Charles Sumner, Oct. 31, 1857 ; d. Sep. 17, 1858. John Simon, Oct. 18, 1860 ; d. July 31, 1861.

† 222. *Bradley,* b. Jan. 29, 1816 ; m. Eunice Aldrich, May 29, 1842, and settled on the homestead in Charlton. She united with the Cong. church by letter, Aug. 1854. The children were : Emily M., Mar. 1843 ; d. Sep. 1843. Charles Edwin, 1849 ; d. a. 4 mos. Lury Ann, Sep. 1850 ; d. a. 5 mos. John, Sep. 1853 ; d. a. 6 mos. Lucy R., Nov. 27, 1854. Sally M., June 4, 1856.

223. *Cathcrine*, b. Dec. 9, 1817 ; m. Harrison Elwell of Dudley, and d. at Bristol, Ct., Dec. 19, 1844, leaving no children.

224. *John Edwin*, b. Jan. 28, 1820 ; d. Oct. 2, 1825.

225. *Mary*, b. Jan. 22, 1822 ; d. Sep. 5, 1825.

226. *Lavina*, b. Mar. 2, 1824 ; m. Theodore Harrington, Oct. 29, 1845 ; settled in Southbridge, Mass, and had Ella J., Mar. 1849 ; Jerome, Dec. 1850.

227. *Lury*, b. Apr. 2. 1826 ; d. Mar. 15, 1833.

† 228. *Havelin Town*, b. Sep. 11, 1828 ; m. Eglantine Aldrich, a sister of Eunice Aldrich, (222) Oct. 31, 1853, and settled in Springfield, Mass., and had Sarah Gilbert, Jan. 7, 1860 ; d. July 23, 1860. William Lewis, Apr. 11, 1866.

229. *Sally A.*, b. Oct. 15, 1830 ; d. Mar. 9, 1833.

220. *Mary Eliza*, b. June 15, 1833 ; m. Schuyler Corlen of Charlton, and had Henry.

VII. 31.-91. MARTIN FITTS married MIRIAM DRESSER, Jan. 20, 1818, at Sempronius, N. Y., where he settled in 1816. She was born in Hinsdale, Mass., Mar. 26, 1793, the daughter of Joseph and Miriam, and died Oct. 15, 1866.

Children born in Sempronius :

231. *Dwight*, b. Mar. 2, 1820 ; d. May 5, 1825.

† 232. *Leander*, b. May 23, 1822 ; m. first, Nov. 2, 1853, Tirza A. Smith of Courtland, N. Y., the dau. of John and Fanny, formerly of Coleraine, Mass., and who d. Feb. 3, 1855 ; m. second, Fanny C. Smith, sister of Tirza A., Sep. 2, 1856, who d. Feb. 11, 1861 ; m. third, Aug. 2, 1864, Mary Smith, dau. of Ezekiel and Louisa of Sempronius, N. Y. Leander Fitts was a teacher, merchant and afterward Cashier of the First National Bank of Moravia, Cayuga Co., N. Y. Issue by first m.: Tirza L., Oct. 10, 1854 ; d. May 30, 1855. Issue by third m.: Twins, son and dau., Mar. 1866.

† 233. *Lucius*, b. Sep. 11, 1824 ; m. Mar. 2, 1847, Isabel Hall, dau. of William and Ann of Sempronius. They settled in Sempronius, and had issue: Francis D., Dec. 26, 1847 ; d. Dec. 30, 1848. Ann H., June 6, 1850. Caroline, Feb. 27, 1852. Alice M., June 12, 1854. George William, Aug. 8, 1856. Fanny, Mar. 28, 1858 ; d. Jan. 11, 1859. Milton L., Feb. 27, 1860. Lurie, Apr. 13, 1862. Fay, Jan. 28, 1865.

† 234. *Julius*, b. July 20, 1827, m. Dec. 30, 1852, Mary Jane Brown, dau. of Daniel and Mary. They settled on the homestead in Sempronius, and had Charlie, Jan. 21, 1854. Alta, May 30, 1861.

235. *Zebina*, b. Mar. 30, 1830 ; d. Feb. 4, 1858.

236. *Mary Ann*, b. Dec. 6, 1832.

VII. 42.-96. JESSE FITTS married HARRIET STONE, Mar. 18, 1816. They resided in Oakham, Mass., where she d. in 1849, and he May 22, 1853.

Their children were :

237. *Catherine Augusta*, b. June 8, 1818 ; m. Daniel Noyes, Dec. 10, 1843, and d. at Oakham, Oct. 9, 1844.

9

† 238. *Jonathan Harvey*, b. Aug. 13, 1821 ; m. Elisabeth Jane Austin, Oct. 15, 1850, and settled in Ashland. Mass Children: Lizzie M., Jan. 19, 1854 ; d. Sep. 26, 1860. George H., Apr. 26, 1862. Arthur M., June 21, 1864.

239. *Harriet Amelia*, b. Mar. 25, 1826 ; m. Wm. A. F. Noyes of Ashland, June 2, 1844, and had Charlotte A., Dec. 6, 1848 ; m. Thomas M. Robinson, June 6, 1866. Twins, Charles F., and Chester S., Sep. 9, 1854.

240. *John Williams*, b. Dec. 13, 1829 ; m. Susan A. Holbrook, lived in Brookfield, and had Benjamin Homer, Apr. 10, 1866.

241. *Mary Abbot*, b. Mar. 14, 1837 ; m. William Clark of Brookfield, Apr. 1, 1855, and had J. Herbert, Nov. 8, 1861.

VII. 42.–99. Elisha Fitts married Zilla Johnson of Oakham, where she died in 1850. He died at Worcester, May 3, 1836 ; a. 37.
Their children were :
242. *George Emery*.
243. *John Appleton*.

VII. 45.–103. Daniel Fitts was married to Lydia Livermore of Auburn, Jan. 17, 1808, by John Prentice, Justice of the Peace. He lived in Charlton, Oxford and Auburn.
The children were :
244. *Tirzah*, b. May 11, 1808 ; m. Price Stoddard.
245. *Emeline*, b. Apr. 9, 1810 ; m. Orson Merrill.
246. *Diantha*, b. Mar. 24, 1813 ; m. ——— Waite.
247. *Lorinda*, b. Apr. 11, 1816 ; m. ——— Meriam.
248. *Elisha Livermore*, b. Jan. 16, 1819 ; d. Apr. 11, 1819.

VII. 45.–107. John Fitts married first, Feb. 14, 1819, Eliza Green, who was born Oct. 9, 1794, and died Aug. 16, 1843. He afterward married, Louisa Vassall, (m. n. Southworth,) Sep. 12, 1844. She had been the second wife of Benjamin Vassall, who was born at Charlton, Feb. 16, 1784 ; m. Apr. 3, 1831, and died May 6, 1843, the son of Lieut. Benjamin Vassall of the Revolution. John Fitts lived in Auburn and Oxford, Mass., and for some time in the State of New York.
Issue by first marriage :
249. *Nancy Clark*, b. Aug. 31, 1820.
250. *Chloe White*, b. June 19, 1823 ; d. July 21, 1825.
251. *Susan Henderson*, b. Oct. 28, 1827 ; m. George Waite.
† 252. *Julius*, b. May 26, 1830 ; m. Sep. 2, 1855, Sally Ann Barnes (m. n. Walker,) the dau. of Ebenezer B., and Roxanna (Wicker) Walker of Oxford, and had Ednah Eliza, Sep. 26, 1856. Addie Louise, Aug. 16, 1859. John Charles Ellsworth, Sep 23, 1862. Edgar Everett, Feb. 18, 1867.

VII. 45.–108. ARBA FITTS married first, MARY HOSMER, published Sep. 27, 1816, and second, JULIA WESSON, published June 27, 1829. He lived in Oxford and Auburn.

"ARBA FITTS,
died Mar. 24, 1858,
aged 61 yrs.

MARY H.,
his wife,
died April, 1828."

Tombstone.

Children by first marriage :
253. *Ira,* b. 1817 ; m. ——— Mullet.
254. *Perry,* b. Aug. 29, 1819 ; m.
255. *Amanda M.,* b. Oct. 6. 1821 ; m. ——— Putnam.
256. *Mary Ann,* b. Apr. 27, 1824 ; d. young.
257. *Amory,* b. May 28, 1825.
258. *Elisabeth,* b. Jan. 29, 1828 ; m. ——— Jay.
Issue by second marriage :
259. *George,* b. Dec. 28, 1829.

———

VII. 46.–112. WALTER FITTS, JR., married 1808 or 1809, MARY COZENS, dau. of John of Oxford. They lived in Oxford, Southbridge and Charlton.
The children were :
260. *Amanda,* b. Jan. 3, 1810 ; d. 1813.
261. *Mary Cozens,* b. Dec. 26, 1811 ; m. Asa Twiss of Charlton, Nov. 4, 1832.
262. *Amanda M.,* b. Aug. 6, 1814 ; m. Nelson McIntire of Charlton.
563. *Celia,* b. May 31, 1817 ; m. John A. Fay of Worcester.
264. *Betsey,* b. July 25, 1819 ; d. Sep. 19, 1822.
265. *Luben O.,* b. Mar. 18, 1822 ; m. Cordelia McCoach, had Arthur L., and d. Feb. 1857.
† 266. *Vernon,* b. Aug. 30, 1824 ; m. Ruth Ann Stevens, settled in Charlton, and had, Fannie C., Sep. 17, 1856. Wilbur, Dec. 27, 1857. Ernest, July 8, 1859. Lelia, May 20, 1861.

———

VII. 46.–115. JONATHAN FITTS married LAMINDA HOBBS, May 1813, who was born at Sturbridge, Sep. 23, 1796. They lived at Holland, Mass., and at Irasburg and Albany, Vt. He was postmaster and carried on " tanning and currying and shoe manufacturing."
Their children were :
267. *Almira,* b. Jan. 25, 1814.
† 268. *Walter Fairfield,* b. Dec. 24, 1815 ; m. Nov. 3, 1842, and had Flavilla B., Sep. 18, 1843. Mary A., Jan. 1846. Sereno W., July 4, 1851.
269. *Heman Allen,* b. Aug. 1, 1826.
270. *Laminda A.,* b. Apr. 22, 1826.
271. *Algena F.,* b. Mar. 27, 1834.

VII. 47.–121. EDWARD FITTS married AMY DRAPER of Brimfield, and settled in Shutesbury, Mass. She died Oct. 6, 1847 ; a. 66. He had a second wife, and died at Pelham, Sep. 19, 1854 ; a. 73.

> " Dear father ! thou art gone and left us,
> Never more thy face to see :
> Thy children dear,
> Now shed the bitter sorrowing tear,
> That death so soon did call.
>
> But fully resigned wast thou to leave
> This world of sin and pain ;
> And since thou wast blest, we will not grieve,
> Nor wish thee back again."

Nine children born in Shutesbury :

272. *Edward*, b. Feb. 10, 1807 ; m. Louisa Chandler and had Henry.

273. *Caleb Draper*, b. Dec. 30, 1808 ; grain merchant, Justice of the Peace, &c., Chicago ; twice m., first to Ellen Paine, by whom he had Ellen Paine ; m. —— Standard and Paine.

274. *Infant son.*

275. *Amy*, m. Charles Philips, and had Adaline ; m. —— Mesler. Susan ; m. —— Seeben.

276. *Mary*, m. Noah Phelps of Shutesbury, and had Jarvis, James.

277. *Infant son.*

278. *Rhoda B.*, b. Aug. 3, 1820 ; m. June 13, 1841, Josiah C. Holton, who was b. Apr. 4, 1819, and had issue : Edward D., Aug. 7, 1844. Marvin B., June 13, 1847 ; d. July 5, 1847.

279. *Phebe*, m. Charles Phelps, a bro. of Noah, lived in Iowa, and had Henry.

280. *Adaline*, m. William Hopkins and settled on the homestead in Shutesbury.

————

VII. 47.–122. RUFUS FITTS married LUCY SANDERSON of Leverett, Oct. 1, 1813, and resided in Charlton and Leverett, Mass., and in Putney, Vt. He was a blacksmith, a licensed preacher of the Baptist profession, a Justice of the Peace, and a Representative to General Court of Mass. from the town of Leverett.

Their children were :

281. *Caroline M.*, b. June 12, 1817 ; m. —— Hatch, and d. before 1865.

282. *Minerva P.*, b. Apr. 28, 1820 ; m. John Knight, and lived in Westmoreland, N. H.

† 283. *Robert B.*, b. July 9, 1822 ; resided in Boston and Philadelphia, Editor of The American Union, Secretary of the North American Mining Company, &c. ; m. first, Dec. 1846, Harriet A. Masters of Manchester, Mass., who d. Mar. 8, 1860 ; m. second, 1865, Hattie —— of Philadelphia, who was b. 1839. Issue by first marriage : Georgianna, d. in infancy. Hattie K., July, 1849. Robert, d. young. Henry Lee. Carrie Louisa.

† 284. *James B.*, b. Sep. 30, 1824 ; m. Viola H. Rice of Wardsboro',
Vt., and d. at Northboro', Mass., 1865, leaving Fred, b. about 1857.
  285. *Rufus H.*, b. Aug. 21, 1830, and lived at Lawrence, Kansas.
  286. *George P.*, b. Dec. 2, 1838, and lived in Canon City, Nevada.

VII. 47.–125. ROBERT FITTS was published to LUCY BANGS of
Hardwick, Sep. 17, 1819, and married, Nov. 1, 1819. She was the
daughter of Elijah and Sarah Bangs. They resided in Auburn, Leicester, Leverett and Northampton. He was connected with the Baptist
church in Auburn, and also with the church in North Oxford at its
organization, Apr. 13, 1837. He was also one of the original members
of the Baptist Society of North Oxford, and was on important committees, 1836, May 5, and June 16 ; 1837 ; 1838, Jan. 11, and Mar. 13.
  The children were :
† 287. *Elijah Bangs*, b. Sep. 24, 1820 ; m. Parmelia C. Field, dau.
of Heman and Acksey, and settled in Amherst. Issue : Heman F.,
Sep. 15, 1847. Robert C., Feb. 1850. Elijah B., 1852. Nathan H.,
Mar. 1855. George F. July, 1860.
  288. *Mary M.*, b. May 30, 1822 ; m. David H. Nutting, settled in
Iowa, and had Sarah L., May 8, 1859.
† 289. *Nathan Haskall*, b. Dec. 23, 1823 ; m. Feb. 2, 1847, Lucy
Moore, dau. of Martin and Beedah of Montague, and had Charles K.,
Feb. 16, 1857. Nathan H., d. Oct. 19, 1858.
  290. *Sarah Lucy*, b. June 26, 1827 ; m. Ansel Wright, the son of
Ansel and Elisabeth of Northampton. Issue : Lizzie B., Feb. 3, 1860.
Fred W., Sep. 11, 1862. Lucy F., Jan. 6, 1864. A daughter, July 6,
1866.
  291. *Hannah Bangs*, b. Dec. 1, 1831 ; m. Nov. 20, 1855, George
B. Wright, a bro. of Ansel. He was merchant, treasurer and collector of Northampton, Sheriff of the County, &c., and d. Nov. 16, 1865 ;
a, 39. Issue : Hattie Elisabeth, Sep. 20, 1857. George F., Sep. 17,
1863.
  292. *Robert*, b. Jan. 14, 1833 ; d. July 12, 1833.

        " Peace to thy dust, dear babe, farewell."

VII. 47.–127. REV. HERVEY FITTZ married first, ANGELINE ANGELL
JENKS, Sep. 14, 1829, by Rev. Addison Parker. She was the oldest
child of Dr. Nicholas and Betsey Jenks, born in West Boylston, Aug.
10, 1810 ; baptized and admitted to the Baptist church in Southbridge,
1823, and died at Middleboro', Sep. 30, 1861. The funeral discourse
which was published, was by Rev. J. G. Warren, D. D., assisted in
the devotional exercises by Rev. A. Pollard, D. D., and Rev. P. L.
Cushing.
  REV. HERVEY FITTZ married for his second wife, HANNAH (WOOD)
LAZELL of Middleboro', 1862.
  Mr. Fittz was baptized in 1823 ; graduated at Amherst, 1826, where
he took the part of "Salutatory," and at Newton, 1829. He was
ordained at Waterville, Me., 1829, and was settled at Waterville and
Hollowell, Me., and at South Boston, Middleboro', Marblehead and
Millbury, Mass. Early in 1843, he was engaged to labor as an agent
of the Mass. Baptist Convention, in which service he remained for a

quarter of a century. Among his published productions was a sermon before the Old Colony Baptist Association, Oct. 1, 1834, and entitled: "Obedience to Christ, the Test of Discipleship." He also wrote a work entitled: "Baptists do not exclude Pedo Baptists but are excluded by them." Also, "An Account of Abraham Vest, or The Castoff Restored."

Issue by first marriage:

† 293. *Edwin Hervey*, b. Oct. 2, 1830; m. Nov. 28, 1854, Elisabeth Ann Tenney of Palmer, b. May 19, 1834, the only dau. of Dea. Eliphalet and Susan M. Tenney. They lived in Palmer and Northboro', Mass., and had George D., Sep. 17, 1864; d. Aug. 14, 1865. Frank Hervey, Oct. 6, 1865.

294. *George Boardman*, b. Mar 2, 1834; a member of Plymouth County Bar.

† 295. *Lonzo Lyon*, b. Dec. 17, 1839; grad. at Brown University, 1861, and at Newton, 1865; ordained at So. Wilbraham, Feb. 1866; m. Fannie Flye, June, 1866; settled at Saginaw City, Mich., June 1867.

206. *Herbert Rogene*, b. May 26, 1850.

VII. 53.-129. ABIJAH WHITING FITTS married ELISABETH PENROW, and lived in Charlton, Mass., and Central Falls, R. I.
Their children were:
297. *Levi*, m. and had children.
298. *Benjamin*, d. 1863; a. 26.
299. *Elisabeth*, m. Rev. Daniel Rounds, a Baptist clergyman, and had William Fitts, 1845. George Marshal, 1856. A daughter, d. young.
300. *A child*, d. in infancy.

VII. 54.-137. CLARK FITTS was published to HANNAH R. PUTNAM of Charlton, Nov. 25, 1831, who was born Dec. 28, 1802, the daughter of Calvin and Abigail (Davidson) Putnam; and died, Apr. 27, 1866. He settled on the "Rich" farm the home of his mother, where he died, May 7, 1866.
Their children were:
301. *Lewis P.*, b. Oct. 1832; d. Dec. 1836.
302. *Emory Clark*, b. Mar. 1, 1837; 'm. Ann Sophia (Sibley) Johnson, Sep. 27, 1866, and settled on the homestead. She was b. Dec. 1844, the dau. of Ira and Sophronia (Shumway) Sibley of Oxford.
303. *William*, d. Dec. 8, 1843; a. 3 days.

VII. 54.-138. ALVIN FITTS of Oxford married LUCY STEVENS, Dec. 14, 1843, by Rev. Mr. Bugbee of Charlton. She was born Sep. 13, 1820, the daughter of John and Lois (Nichols) Stevens of Charlton.
Their children were:
304. *John Stevens*, b. June 9, 1845.
305. *George*, b. Dec. 19, 1847.
306. *Mary Lucy*, b Apr. 23, 1849.
307. *Ann Minerva*, b. Feb. 28, 1854.
308. *Sarah Jane*, b. Jan. 8, 1860.

VII. 54.-139. DAVID FITTS married CHLOE NICHOLS, Aug. 7, 1832, and settled at the "County Gore" in Oxford. She was born, Feb. 8, 1812, the daughter of John P., and Sophia (Shumway) Nichols of Charlton.

Their children were:
309. *A son*, d. in infancy, Apr. 14, 1834.
310. *Hollis*, b. Oct. 9, 1836; d. Sep. 15, 1839.
311. *Jotham*, b. Dec. 17, 1840.
312. *Benjamin*, b. Oct. 31, 1842.
313. *Chloe Ann*, b. Dec. 5, 1846.

VII. 54.-140. LEWIS FITTS married NANCY MINERVA JENNISON of Auburn, published Apr. 6, 1833.

Their children were:
314. *Sarah Minerva*, m. David Lilley of Oxford, and d. Apr. 25, 1859; a. 25.
315. *Albert Lewis*, b. Oct. 8, 1836; m. Lorinda Brooks of Charlton, lived in Worcester, and had Albert Jefferson, Aug. 18, 1855; d. in infancy. Lewis R., July 10, 1857. Sarah Lorraine, Aug. 10, 1860; d. May 6, 1864.
316. *Lillie Jennison*, b. July 17, 1838; d. Aug. 22, 1838.
317. *Levi*, d. in infancy.

VII. 54.-141. HARRISON FITTS married NANCY HOUSTON, the daughter of William of Ontario, N. Y., and settled in Rollin, Mich.

The children were:
318. *Ruth Augusta.*
319. *Vernelia.*
320. *Lewis Cass.*
321. *Sarah.*
322. *Charles.*
323. *William.*
324. *Mary.*

VII. 56.-143. BENJAMIN FITTS married AURELIA PRISTOL of Palmyra, N. Y., and lived in Toledo, Ohio.

The children were:
325. *George Albert.*
326. *J*, b. Aug. 1853.

VII. 56.-145. SUMNER FITTS married first, VERNELIA WHITNEY of Ontario, N. Y., and lived in New York and at Manassas Junction, Va.

Issue:
327. *Edgar Eugene*, b. Aug. 4, 1849.

Mr. Fitts married for his second wife, 1854, MARY WILEY of Walworth, N. Y., by whom he had issue:
328. *Charles.*

VII.   56.–150. Andrew Nelson Fitts married Maria Whitney, the sister of Vernelia of Ontario, N. Y., and lived in Lincoln, formerly Walworth, Wayne Co., N. Y.

Issue :

329.   *Alberto.*
330.   *Mary Louisa.*

VII.   60.–152. Silas Fitts married Lucetta B. Larkin, Aug. 16, 1835, by Rev. Loring Robbins, pastor of the Cong. church in Oxford, and settled in Oxford and Clinton, Mass. She was born at Lancaster, Oct. 11, 1818.

Their children were :

† 331.   *William Ebenezer,* b. July 25, 1837 ; m. Clara A. Knight of Fitchburg, Mar. 23, 1857 ; d. at Clinton, Mar. 18, 1865, and had George Franklin, Aug. 20, 1857. Silas Ariosto, Oct. 20, 1859 ; d. Nov. 17, 1859. Lillie Mabel, Oct. 19, 1860. Adrianne, Dec. 16, 1862.

332.   *Elisabeth,* b. Apr. 26, 1838 ; m. Alfred B. Newton, Feb. 14, 1857, the son of A. P. Newton and of Sophia (Fitts) Adams (102), and had Isaac Herbert ; Ann Lucetta ; Willie.

333.   *Daniel,* b. June 10, 1840 ; m. Theressa Maria Hodges, May 8, 1863, a sister of Laura Ann (154,) and had Carrie Theresa, Feb. 23, 1864.

334.   *Palmer,* b. Feb. 18, 1842 ; m. Emily L. Jewett, July 2, 1864.
335.   *Ann Lucetta,* d. Oct. 1, 1850 ; a. 8 mos. 7 dys.
336.   *Dacy Adaliue,* b. Nov. 11, 1852.

VII.   60.–154. Linus Fitts married Laura Ann Hodges, July 21, 1855, and settled in Clinton, Mass. She was born in Moria, N. Y., the daughter of Jonah and Judith (Bean) Hodges.

Their children were :

337.   *A son,* d. Dec. 27, 1857.
338.   *Walter Edgar,* b. May 28, and d. Aug. 29, 1859.
339.   *James Leslie,* b. Mar. 3, and d. Sep. 2, 1861.

VII.   60.–156. Levi Fitts married Prudence Balcom of Douglass, Sep. 24, 1848, and lived in East Douglass, Mass. She was born Mar. 29, 1828.

The children were :

340.   *George Edwin,* b. Oct. 10, 1850.
341.   *Emma Jane,* b. Apr. 22, 1855.
342.   *Alice Amelia,* b. Oct. 20, 1857.
343.   *Willie Francis,* b. Oct. 22, 1860.
344.   *Elmer Wellington,* b. Nov. 23, 1862.

VII.   63.–158. Charles Fitts married Asenath Blood of Charlton, Mass., 1812, and lived in Groton and Dryden, N. Y., where he died, Jan. 14, 1837. She was living in 1866, at the age of 85.

•

Their children were:

345. *Leonard*, b. Sep. 10, 1813 ; m. Julia A. Harrington of Dryden, Sep. 10, 1841, and had Charles T., Sep. 1, 1842 ; m. Saloma Cummings of Milan, Mar. 15, 1866. Henry W., Feb. 24, 1844 ; d. in the army at Lookout Valley, Tenn., Feb. 11, 1864. Alonzo, Sep. 23, 1846. Mary, Aug. 20, 1853.

346. *Edwin*, b. Aug. 1816 ; m. Mary E. Birthrong of Dryden, Oct. 1856, and had Jessie, Oct. 10, 1856. Sophia, Apr. 15, 1861. John, Dec 9, 1863.

347. *Horace*, b. Mar. 24, 1824 ; m. Mary Jane Griswold, May 9, 1849, and had Frances A., July 11, 1850. Charles S., Sep. 28, 1852.

348. *Angeline.*

VII. 63.–164. CALEB FITTS of Charlton, Mass., married first, SARAH STEVENS of Charlton, and second, LYDIA STEVENS, who was born Sep. 12, 1807, and published Dec. 10, 1831.

Issue by first marriage :

349. *A daughter*, d. in infancy.

Issue by second marriage :

350. *Jerome*, b. Oct. 30, 1832.

351. *Charles H.*, b. Oct. 27, 1834 ; m. Mary Ann Brooks of Charlton; pub. Oct. 26, 1859, and lived in Brookfield.

352. *Sarah A.*, b. June 5, 1837 ; m. Emery Southwick of Charlton.

353. *Russel*, b. Apr. 15, 1839.

354. *Leonard*, b. Jan. 8, 1841.

355. *Lucinda*, b. Mar. 8, 1843 ; m. Francis Dody, lived in Charlton, and had children.

356. *Olive Jane*, b. Aug. 24, 1847.

VII. 63.–166. ANDREW PATCH FITTS married June 16, 1833, SARAH BACON, who was born at Brimfield, Mass., Sep. 14, 1804. He was killed on the railroad at Worcester, Dec. 9, 1850.

Their children were:

357. *Sarah Maria*, b. Apr. 28, 1834 ; d. June 15, 1839.

358. *Mary Jane*, b. Oct. 4, 1835 ; d. Oct. 8, 1836.

359. *Lyman*, b. Oct. 17, 1836.

360. *Alfred,*, b. May, 21, 1838 ; d. Oct. 21, 1838.

361. *Winfield Scott*, b. Dec. 21, 1839 ; m. Henrietta Burlingame, and had children.

362. *Henry H.*, b. Apr. 4, 1842 ; d. Aug. 21, 1843.

VII. 65.–168. LEVI FITTS married Nov. 19, 1822, ARTENE CLARK, the daughter of James and Elisabeth (Duncan) Clark of Jamaica, Vt. He represented the town of Wardsboro', Vt., in the Legislatue of 1849 and 1850.

Their children were:

363. *Rosella C.*, b. Sep. 19, 1823 ; m. James M. Burnham, Mar. 12, 1844, and d. Oct. 6, 1844.

364. *Serecta A.*, b. Nov. 4, 1824 ; m. Apr. 27, 1846, James M. Burnham, and d. Mar. 4, 1847, leaving Serecta R., b. Feb. 22, 1847.

365. *Lauretta L.*, b. Nov. 27, 1828 ; m. Darwin A. Hammond, July 3, 1850, and had issue : Fred A., Aug. 8, 1851. Clara A., Mar. 25, 1855. Edbert D., Aug. 7, 1857. Arthur E., June 25, 1861.

† 366. *Osmer C.*, b. Aug. 13, 1830 ; m. Abbie M. Twitchell, June 4, 1864 ; settled in West Wardsboro', where he was selectman, 1860, 1861 ; assessor, 1862, 1863 ; postmaster, 1867, and had Mary Frances, Apr. 7, 1865.

367. *Philura M.*, b. Feb. 26, 1833 ; m. Thomas F. Johnson, May 21, 1851, and had issue : Lura L., July 26, 1852. Jennie T., July 11, 1855. Mary Annette, June 18, 1857. Levi Caleb, Sep. 11, 1859 ; d. Nov. 30, 1863. Albert E., June 30, 1862 ; d. Aug. 10, 1865. Calla C., May 5, 1864. •

VII. 65.–170. AMASA FITTS married ELIZA WARD, Apr. 25, 1825, and settled at South Wardsboro', Vt., a farmer and postmaster. She was born at Wardsboro', the daughter of Nathaniel and Cynthia (Clark) Ward of Holliston, Mass. Her father Nathaniel represented Wardsboro' in the Legislature. Her grandfather Theophilus Clark was killed at Ticonderoga in the French war.

Their children were :

368. *Stearns A.*, b. Feb. 3, 1826, and lived in Ohio.

369. *Angeline M.*, b. Jan. 30, 1828 ; m. Hiram B. Kidder of Wardsboro', May 30, 1850, and had Jennie, Feb. 5, 1851. Ella, July 19, 1858.

370. *Nathaniel*, b. and d. 1830.

† 371. *Albert*, b. Aug. 16, 1831 ; m. Mrs. Cerintha Kilburn, Aug. 31, 1864; settled in Dummerston, Vt., and had Edgar A., Aug. 29, 1865.

372. *Mary E.*, b. Jan. 26, 1835 ; m. Spencer Robinson, Sep. 27, 1854, and had Alma E., Sep. 21, 1856. Lizzie A., Apr. 19. 1860. Hattie M., Jan. 19, 1863. Willie S., Aug. 22, 1866.

† 373. *Elmer*, b. July 22, 1838 ; m. Cynthia Ann Hambleton, July 29, 1863 ; lived in California, and had Angie M., June 19, 1866.

374. *Emily S.*, b. July 30, 1840 ; m. Charles H. Rice, Sep. 15, 1864.

375. *Oscar Amasa*, b. Sep. 9, 1843.

376. *Frederick F.*, b. June 6, 1847 ; d. June 1, 1855.

VII. 65.–171. EBENEZER FITTS married MATILDA MORSE of Newfane, Vt., Dec. 6, 1827, and settled on the homestead in Wardsboro', where he died July 19, 1847

Their children were :

† 377. *Henry 'N.*, b. Nov. 24, 1828 ; m. Jane L. Newell, May 10, 1849, was selectman and representative of Wardsboro', 1862, 1863, and had Elwin, Aug. 28, 1852. Cora E., Jan. 15, 1862.

378. *Lucy*, b. Sep. 13, 1830 ; d. Oct. 25, 1833.

379. *Marcia*, b. Nov. 15, 1832 ; m. Merrick J. Dowley, Dec. 24, 1851, and d. Nov. 30, 1852.

380. *Luanna,* b. Oct. 24, 1834 ; m. Lucius Lyman, Oct. 15, 1855, and settled on the homestead.

381. *Edwin,* b. Apr. 8, 1837 ; d. Feb. 28, 1839.

382. *Edward,* b. Oct. 28, 1839 ; enlisted into Berdan's Regiment of sharp shooters, and died at Washington, D. C., Oct. 6, 1861.

383. *Rosella,* b. Aug. 19, 1845.

Maine Branch.

FOURTH GENERATION.

IV. 5.–20. "Samuel Fitts of Ips., and Mary Beadle of York, pub. 3ᵈ day Dec. 1726."

In 1724, Mar. 27, he was appointed guardian " unto Ebenezer Fitts, a minor of about seventeen years of age, son of Abraham Fitts, late of sᵈ Ipswich, decᵈ." He was afterward a chairmaker settled in Kittery, Me.

Their children were eight sons and three daughters :

† 21. *John*, b. 1733 ; d. Mar. 24, 1808 ; a. 75.

22. *Ebenezer.*

23. *Benjamin*, probably m. ——— Cutts, was a turner at Kittery, where he received a deed of land from Samuel Fitts, May 21, 1770.

24. *Obediah.*

25. *Ephraim*, m. and settled in Bath, and had A daughter, m. ——— Johnson of Cambridge, Mass. A daughter, m. ——— Donnel of Windham, Me.

26. *Samuel*, a turner of Kittery, and gave a deed 1755, Mar. 17 ; also another to Benjamin Fitts. 1770, May 21.

† 27. *Simeon*, settled in Scarboro', Me.

28. *Simon*, a chairmaker of Scarboro', and gave deed of land 1765, Oct. 29.

29. *Mary.*

30. *Mercy*, m. ——— Chute.

31. *Lucy*, m. Simeon Milliken.

FIFTH GENERATION.

V. 20.–21. John Fitts married Eleanor Googins, who died Apr. 13, 1811 ; a. 70. He was a chairmaker in Saco, Me., 1760, as appears by Folsom's History of Saco and Biddeford, p. 263, and moved to Freeport, then North Yarmouth in 1768, where he died Mar. 24, 1808 ; a. 75.

Their children were:

† 32. *Samuel*, b. Nov. 28, 1768.

33. *Mary*, d. Feb. 7, 1843; a. 71 yrs. 6 mos.

34. *Richard*, unm.; d Jan. 25, 1847; a. 71 yrs. 2 mos.

35. *Eleanor*, d. Aug. 31, 1805; a. 28.

36. *John*, d. young.

37. *Ebenezer*, killed by the falling of a chimney when he was ten years of age.

38. *Others*, d. in infancy.

————

V. 20.–27. SIMEON FITTS married and settled as a chairmaker in Scarboro', Me., where he was grantor or grantee in conveyances of land by deeds, 1763, July 5; 1770, Aug. 3; 1772, Sep. 13, *et als.* Nov. 26, 1774, he gave a deed to John Thompson, Jr, of Scarboro', of Lot No. 15, Range E, 2d Division in the town of Buxton, which he says he purchased of Dea. Jeremiah Bragdon late of York.

Issue:

39. *Mary*, b. Apr. 13, 1775; m. Christopher Holmes, June 4, 1802, and was living at Portland in 1868.

† 40. *Ebenezer*, b. 1780; twice married.

41. *Eunice*, m. John Foster and d. at Castine 1862, leaving no children.

42. *Others*, d. young.

•

SIXTH GENERATION.

VI. 21.–32. SAMUEL FITTS married ELEANOR GOOGINS of Saco, Feb. 15, 1815, who was born June 13, 1792. He was the only member of the family who married, and he was 46 at the time of marriage. He also married his cousin by the same name of his mother. They settled in Freeport where all their ten children except John also lived.

† 43. *Ebenezer*, b. May 4, 1816; m. Eunice Tuttle, July 10, 1840, and d. Feb. 20, 1853, having had children: Edwin, July 23, 1841; m. Ellen L. Brackett, Jan. 7, 1867. Woodbury, Oct. 18, 1844; m. Abbie N. Davis, Dec. 7, 1865, and had Fred W., Sep. 2, 1866.

44. *Samuel*, b. Oct. 31, 1817.

45. *Susan*, b. Apr. 3, 1820; m. Joseph Davis, Oct. 21, 1841.

46. *Eleanor*, b. Mar. 31, 1822.

47. *John*, b. Apr. 20, 1824; lived for a time in Portland. In a deed to which he was a party, May 18, 1850, he is called a joiner of Freeport.

48. *Mary*, b. Feb. 23, 1826.

49. *Elisabeth J.*, b. May 5, 1828; m. James T. Tuttle, Nov. 14, 1847.

50. *Joseph G.*, b. Sep. 22, 1830.

51. *Almira*, b. June 4, 1833.

52. *Simeon Philip*, b. June 5, 1836; d. Aug. 22, 1838.

VI. 27.–40. EBENEZER FITZ married first, MARY ——— in Kennebunk, by whom he had one child, that died young in Castine. Married second, NANCY ANN PRUDEN. A deed to which he was a party in 1802, Nov. 18, is signed Ebenezer Fitz, Pepperelborough, cordwainer, and Mary Fitz his wife. Another dated, Oct. 4, 1817, is signed Ebenezer Fitz, Castine, barber, and Nancy Ann Fitz his wife. He died at Castine, Mar. 1851.

Issue by second marriage:

† 53. *Eben P.,* m. and lived at Norway, Oxford Co., Me., where he affixed his name to a deed, Feb. 16, 1864.

54. *Charles T.,* a tin plate and sheet iron worker at Castine, where he had a wife living in 1868. His name occurs in connection with conveyances of real estate, 1855, Oct. 11 ; 1856, Oct. 21.

55. *Mary,* d. young.

INDEXES.

CHRISTIAN NAMES.

The figures refer to pages. The repetition of a name on the same page is not indicated.

A

Aaron, 32, 34, 35, 36, 37, 39, 64.
Abbie Ide, 49.
Abbie Lucinda, 40.
Abby Ann, 40.
Abby Manly, 25.
Abel, 9, 13, 14, 15, 16.
Abel Brown, 15.
Abigail, 4, 6, 7, 8, 12, 31, 32, 33, 34, 38.
Abigail Ruhamah, 30.
Abijah, 56.
Abijah Whiting, 58, 70.
Abraham, 1, 2, 3, 4, 8, 10, 11, 21, 22, 23, 25, 26, 31, 42, 43, 50, 53, 57, 76.
Ada Busford, 63.
Adaline, 59, 68.
Adda S., 27.
Addie Louise, 66.
Addie May, 14.
Adelaide Eliza, 26.
Adeline Celesta, 28.
Adrianne, 72.
Albert, 39, 48, 74.
Albert E., 74.
Albert Jefferson, 71.
Albert Lewis, 71.
Alberto, 72.
Alfred, 23, 37, 73.
Alfred Dana, 22.
Alfred Metcalf, 18.
Alfred William, 40.
Algena F., 67.
Alice Amelia, 72.
Alice Caroline, 26.

Alice Jenniss, 28.
Alice M., 65.
Alice Malvina, 64.
Almeria Euphratia, 30.
Almira, 13, 17, 43, 47, 67, 77.
Almira B., 43.
Almira L., 44.
Alonzo, 73.
Alta, 65.
Alvin, 58, 70.
Alvin W., 18.
Amanda, 67.
Amanda Louisa, 48.
Amanda M., 67.
Amasa, 60, 74.
Amory, 67.
Amos Knowles, 23.
Amy, 68.
Amzi Wilson, 44.
Anna, 3, 4, 6, 7, 17, 19, 29, 53, 54, 57.
Anna Barnes, 37.
Anna Jane, 37.
Anna S., 44.
Anna Stone, 38.
Anne, 2, 51.
Andrew, 32, 34, 37, 52, 58.
Andrew Jackson, 20.
Andrew Morgan, 37.
Andrew Nelson, 59, 72.
Andrew P., 59.
Andrew Patch, 60, 73.
Angelia L., 64.
Angelina Rebecca, 62.
Angeline, 73.
Angeline M., 74.
Angie M., 74.

Ann Caroline, 29.
Ann H., 65.
Annie Frances, 43.
Annie Hazen, 18.
Ann Louisa, 20, 28.
Ann Lucetta, 72.
Ann Maria, 44, 63.
Ann Minerva, 70.
Ann Rebecca, 64.
Ann Stewart, 25.
Ann Stickney, 34.
Ansel, 45.
Arba, 56, 67.
Artemas, 54.
Arthur E., 74.
Arthur Green, 28.
Arthur L., 28, 67.
Arthur M., 65.
Arthur Salisbury, 40.
Asa, 24.
Asahel, 63.
Asel, 54.
Ashel, 63.
Ashel Eliott, 63.

B

Bella T., 61.
Benaiah, 26.
Benjamin, 12, 21, 27, 28, 43, 50, 52, 58, 70, 71, 76.
Bethia, 31, 33, 34.
Betsey, 9, 15, 36, 56, 67.
Bradford, 63.
Bradley, 64.

C

Caleb, 53, 59, 60, 73.
Caleb Draper, 68.
Calla C., 74.
Calvin Richards, 49.
Carlos Eustace, 26.
Caroline, 56, 62, 63, 65.
Caroline Frances, 14, 28.
Caroline Louisa, 16.
Caroline M., 68.
Carrie Evelyn, 26.
Carrie Louisa, 68.
Carrie Sleeper, 16.
Carrie Theresa, 72.
Catherine, 65.
Catherine Augusta, 65.
Catherine Brown, 21.
Celia, 56, 67.
Charles, 14, 28, 35, 36, 39, 59, 71, 72.
Charles Abel, 14.
Charles Albion, 26.

Charles Austin, 49.
Charles B., 44.
Charles Curtis, 44.
Charles Edwin, 28, 64.
Charles Francis, 48.
Charles Frederick, 18, 22, 25
Charles H., 18, 27, 73.
Charles Harrison, 49.
Charles Hazen, 18.
Charles K., 69.
Charles Morton, 28.
Charles Norton, 28.
Charles S., 73.
Charles Sumner, 64.
Charles T., 73, 78.
Charles William, 37, 41.
Charlie, 65.
Charlie A., 16.
Charlotte, 14, 45, 48,
Charlotte, Coleman, 23.
Charlotte Delia, 48.
Charlotte T., 19.
Charlotte Temple, 13.
Chellis, 16.
Chloe, 56, 60.
Chloe Ann, 71.
Chloe White, 66.
Christianna, 46, 47.
Christopher Columbus, 27.
Clara A., 74.
Clara Morgan, 37.
Clarence Frank, 26.
Clarissa, 24, 60.
Clark, 54, 58, 70.
C. Maria, 45.
Convers, 17.
Cora E., 74.
Cora L., 16.
Cornelia, 45.
Currier, 14, 16.
Curtis Bliss, 45.
Curtis Harvey, 45.
Cynthia, 13, 14, 58.
Cynthia D., 16.
Cyrus, 13.

D

Dacy Adaline, 72.
Daniel, 6, 7, 8, 9, 11, 12, 13, 14, 15, 16, 18, 20, 21, 42, 43, 47, 52, 55, 56, 66, 72.
Daniel Brainard, 25.
Daniel Francis, 14.
Daniel French, 18.
Daniel Poland, 37.
Daniel R., 37.
Daniel Webster, 16.

David, 33, 43, 46, 47, 49, 52, 57, 58, 71.
David B., 44.
David Bucklin, 48.
David Grundie, 45.
David S., 44.
Davis D., 27.
Deborah, 51.
Delany Melissa, 43.
Delia, 47.
Dexter, 18.
Dexter W., 63.
Diantha, 66.
Dorothy, 9, 11, 25, 26, 44.
Dorothy A., 44
Drusilla, 18, 19.
Duty, 43.
Dwight, 65.

E

Ebenezer, 3, 4, 15, 50, 52, 53, 59, 60, 74, 76, 77, 78.
Ebenezer Fuller, 43.
Eben P., 78.
Eber, 55.
Edbert D., 74.
Edgar A., 74.
Edgar Eugene, 71.
Edgar Everett, 66.
Edith, 39.
Edmund Henry, 44.
Edna, 27.
Edna Eliza, 66.
Edson, 26.
Edward, 52, 57, 63, 68, 75.
Edward Appleton, 18.
Edward B., 44.
Edward Dearborn, 27.
Edward Eustace, 40.
Edward Henry, 23.
Edward L., 64.
Edward Payson, 49.
Edward Southworth, 28.
Edwin, 73, 75, 77.
Edwin A., 64.
Edwin Cyrus, 14.
Edwin Franklin, 48.
Edwin Hervey, 70.
Eleanor, 40, 58, 60, 77.
Elias, 24.
Elijah B., 69.
Elijah Bangs, 69.
Elijah T., 63.
Elisabeth, 7, 8, 9, 10, 11, 12, 17, 18, 21, 28, 32, 33, 35, 38, 39, 43, 44, 59, 64, 67, 70, 72, 77.
Elisabeth A., 16.
Elisabeth Ann, 45.

Elisabeth Ann Hall, 21.
Elisabeth Augusta, 30.
Elisabeth Campbell, 35.
Elisabeth Davenport, 37.
Elisabeth H., 29.
Elisabeth K., 18.
Elisabeth S., 44.
Elisha, 55, 66.
Elisha Livermore, 66.
Eliza, 24, 63, 64.
Eliza Ann, 24, 37, 38.
Eliza C., 63.
Eliza Roberts, 39.
Eliza S., 44.
Ella A., 44.
Ella Louisa, 29.
Ellen, 38, 45, 63.
Ellen Augusta, 16.
Ellen Eliza, 25.
Ellen Maria, 28.
Ellen Montgomery, 26.
Ellen Paine, 68.
Ellis M., 64.
Elmer, 74.
Elmer Wellington, 72.
Elwin, 74.
Emeline, 16, 57, 58, 62, 66.
Emeline Delorus, 63.
Emeline R., 44.
Emerson, 45.
Emily, 43.
Emily C., 18.
Emily Hammond, 44.
Emily Jane, 21, 44.
Emily M., 64.
Emily S., 74.
Emily Sarah Green, 28.
Emma, 64.
Emma Frances, 48.
Emmagene, 26.
Emma Jane, 72.
Emma Jennie, 40.
Emory Clark, 70.
Ephraim, 4, 7, 9, 10, 17, 19, 76.
Ernest, 67.
Eugene, 37.
Eunice, 12, 33, 36, 43, 44, 51, 52, 54.
Eunice Augusta, 37.
Eunice Sophronia, 45.
Eustace C., 40.
Eustace Carey, 39.
Eva, 18.
Eveline A., 44,
Ezekiel, 8, 9, 35.

F

Fannie, 58.
Fannie C., 67.

Fanny, 65.
Fay, 65.
Flavilla B., 67.
Florence, 23.
Florence M., 20.
Frances, 15, 64.
Frances A., 73.
Frances Marion, 14.
Frances Place, 19.
Francis, 27, 39, 63.
Francis D., 65.
Francis Dean, 63.
Francis Larkin, 37.
Frank Eugene, 26.
Frank Eustace, 40.
Frank Herbert, 49.
Frank Hervey, 70.
Frank Leroy, 28.
Frank Richard, 16.
Frank Russell, 28.
Frank W., 27.
Franklin, 14, 23, 38, 39.
Fred, 63, 69.
Fred A., 74.
Fred W., 77.
Frederick, 22, 37, 43.
Frederick Augustus, 48.
Frederick F., 74.
Friend P., 44.

G

George, 15, 16, 21, 31, 32, 34, 38, 43,
    48, 54, 61, 62, 63, 67, 70.
George Albert, 41, 71.
George Bartlett, 48.
George Boardman, 70.
George Calvin, 28.
George Coelebs, 62.
George Currier, 14.
George D., 70.
George Dana, 22.
George Edward, 38.
George Edwin, 72.
George Emery, 66.
George Ephraim, 19.
George F., 69.
George Franklin, 72.
George Frederick, 43.
George H., 66.
George Hamilton, 44.
George Hammond, 13.
George Henry, 38, 46.
George Lendrum, 14.
George P., 63, 69.
George Pike, 58.
George W., 13, 19, 44, 61, 64.
George Ware, 37.
George Washington, 28, 45.

George William, 65
Georgia L., 61.
Georgianna, 68.
Gertrude, 57.
Grace, 1.
Grace D., 1.

H

Hannah, 9, 12, 27, 32, 33, 34, 38, 50,
    51, 52.
Hannah Bangs, 69.
Hannah Byenton, 15, 16.
Hannah Elisabeth, 16.
Hannah Godfrey, 26.
Hannah H., 28.
Hannah Lane, 23.
Hannah Philena, 18.
Harriet, 21, 37, 46, 58.
Harriet A., 44.
Harriet Alvira, 16.
Harriet Amelia, 66.
Harriet E., 13.
Harriet Elisabeth, 13.
Harriet Eliza, 44.
Harriet Patience, 45.
Harrison, 20, 58, 71.
Harvey, 45.
Hattie K., 68.
Havelin Town, 65.
Hellen A., 27.
Hellen Johnson, 37.
Hellen Kimball, 14.
Hellen Louisa, 18, 29.
Heman Allen, 67.
Heman F., 69.
Henrietta Caroline, 29.
Henry, 35, 37, 39, 63.
Henry Eugene, 37.
Henry H., 73.
Henry Lee, 68.
Henry Lyman, 49.
Henry M., 44.
Henry Martyn, 43.
Henry N., 74.
Henry T., 18.
Henry Thomas, 18.
Henry W., 73.
Herbert Rogene, 70.
Hervey, 57, 69.
Hiram, 14, 16, 17.
Hollis, 71.
Homer, 16, 26.
Honora, 61.
Horace, 73.
Horace Lucian, 18.
Howard Whittier, 40.
Huldah, 52.

I

Ina Frances, 37.
Ira, 67.
Irving P., 18.
Isaac, 3, 5, 7, 10, 19, 21, 27, 31, 32, 35, 38, 42, 53, 61.
Isaac Jones, 27.
Isaac Newton, 25, 61.
Isabella Bucklin, 48.
Isabel Henrietta, 29.
Isaiah, 12, 29.
Israel, 43, 45.

J

J, 71.
James, 4, 31, 32, 33, 42, 43, 45, 57.
James Ames, 28.
James B., 69.
James Franklin, 22.
James Gale, 20.
James Gilman, 19.
James Hill, 23.
James Leslie, 72.
James M., 16.
James Smith, 48.
James Sumner, 49.
Jennie T., 74.
Jeremiah, 31, 32, 33, 35, 36, 38, 39, 42.
Jerome, 73.
Jerome Colvert, 63.
Jerusha, 6, 8.
Jesse, 55, 65.
Jesse E., 39.
Jesse Remington, 26.
Jessie, 73.
J. George, 16.
Joanna, 17, 36, 60.
John, 4, 23, 29, 31, 32, 33, 34, 35, 36, 38, 40, 42, 44, 51, 53, 54, 56, 62, 63, 64, 66, 73, 76, 77.
John Appleton, 66.
John Charles Ellsworth, 66.
John D., 27.
John Dearborn, 28.
John Edmund, 40.
John Edwin, 65.
John F., 44.
John Frank, 11, 21.
John J., 44.
John James, 45.
John Lane, 23, 25.
John M., 18.
John Meade, 38.
John Milton, 25.
John Mitchell, 13.
John Prescott, 30.
John Simon, 64.

John Stephen, 46.
John Stevens, 70.
John W., 17.
John Williams, 66.
John W. M., 16.
Jonathan, 7, 9, 17, 50, 51, 52, 55, 56, 67.
Jonathan Harvey, 66.
Joseph, 8, 12, 16, 18, 21, 30, 43.
Joseph Bucklin, 49.
Joseph Dennis, 49.
Joseph Edwin, 63.
Joseph Francis, 43.
Joseph G., 77.
Joseph Lamson, 37.
Joseph Warren, 37.
Josephine M., 44.
Joshua, 23.
Josiah, 10, 20, 32, 33, 34, 37.
Josiah Monroe, 20.
Jotham, 56, 71.
Judith, 35, 53.
Judith Bell Currier, 19.
Judith Hall, 21.
Julia A., 16.
Julius, 65, 66.
Julius Augustus, 49.

K

Kate Isabella, 64.
Kezia A., 61.
Keziah, 51.

L

Laminda A., 67.
Laura, 46, 60.
Laura Ann, 18, 46.
Laura Frances, 45.
Lauretta L., 74.
Lauretta M., 61.
Lavina, 65.
Lavinia, 17.
Leafy, 61.
Leander, 65.
Lelia, 67.
Leonard, 36, 40, 60, 73.
Leroy Benson, 18.
Leverett E., 44.
Levi, 58, 59, 60, 70, 71, 72, 73.
Levi Caleb, 74.
Lewis, 58, 71.
Lewis Cass, 71.
Lewis Challis, 16.
Lewis Francis, 43.
Lewis Gilbert, 45.
Lewis L., 64.

Lewis P., 70.
Lewis R., 71.
Lillie Jennison, 71.
Lillie Mabel, 72.
Linus, 59, 72.
Lizzie M., 66.
Lois, 12, 53.
Lonzo Lyon, 70.
Lorenzo R., 18.
Lorinda, 66.
Louisa Adams, 14.
Louisa Isabella, 25.
Louisa M., 30.
Louisa Town, 64.
Luanna, 75.
Luben O., 67.
Lucian, 43.
Lucien, 19.
Lucina, 16, 60.
Lucina W., 62.
Lucinda, 58, 73.
Lucius, 43, 65.
Lucy, 12, 32, 38, 51, 74, 76.
Lucy A., 61, 63.
Lucy Ann, 63.
Lucy B., 62.
Lucy Maria, 45.
Lucy Moore Town, 64
Lucy R., 64.
Luella, 37.
Luella T., 41.
Luke G., 62.
Lurie, 65.
Lury, 55, 64, 65.
Lury Ann, 64.
Lury Jane, 63.
Luther, 28, 29.
Luther Francis, 28.
Lydia, 7, 10, 11, 17, 24, 25, 43, 45, 53, 61.
Lydia Ann, 59.
Lydia Lizebeth, 28.
Lyman, 15, 16, 43, 62, 73.
Lyman Bezer, 62.

M

Mahala, 21.
Marcia, 74.
Margarett, 4, 50, 51.
Margarett Blanchard, 37.
Maria, 19, 46.
Maria Blanchard, 13.
Marietta Williams, 62.
Marion, 14.
Mark, 32, 34, 38.
Martha, 5, 7, 9, 14, 21, 44, 54, 57.
Martha Ann, 22.
Martha Elisabeth, 15.

Martin, 55, 56, 65.
Mary, 4, 6, 7, 9, 10, 12, 13, 20, 21, 27, 28, 32, 33, 34, 36, 38, 42, 43, 44, 48, 50, 51, 52, 55, 56, 59, 60, 65, 68, 71, 73, 76, 77, 78.
Mary A. 18, 67.
Mary Abbie, 24.
Mary Abbot, 66.
Mary Adelaide, 29.
Mary Ann, 13, 10, 20, 28, 45, 63, 65, 67.
Mary Annette, 74.
Mary Augusta, 37.
Mary B., 13.
Mary C., 20, 44.
Mary Catherine, 46.
Mary Cozens, 67.
Mary Cutler, 48.
Mary E., 16, 59, 74.
Mary Elisabeth, 37, 38.
Mary Eliza, 65.
Mary Emma, 26.
Mary Frances, 18, 74.
Mary H., 67.
Mary Harrison, 23.
Mary J., 16, 44.
Mary Jane, 14, 25, 37, 41, 44, 45, 63, 73.
Mary Josephine, 19.
Mary Locke, 29.
Mary Louisa, 48, 59, 72.
Mary Lucy, 70.
Mary M., 69.
Mary T., 61.
May Elisabeth, 63.
Mehitable, 6, 50, 52.
Mehitable Ann, 21.
Melinda, 62.
Melvin H., 44.
Mercy, 4, 8, 50, 52, 76.
Milton L., 65.
Minerva P., 68.
Minnie M., 44.
Miranda Lois, 63.
Miriam, 12, 56.
Miriam Morrill, 29.
Molly, 53.
Monroe Gale, 20.
Morgan Coleman, 48.
Morton, 44.
Moses, 11, 12, 22, 29, 32, 33, 43, 44.
Moses Hall, 22.

N

Nancy, 9, 13, 16, 36, 37, 43, 45, 62.
Nancy Ann, 78.
Nancy Clark, 66.
Nancy Maria, 21.

Nancy S., 16.
Nathan, 8, 11. 12, 26, 28, 29.
Nathan Corydon, 26.
Nathan D., 27.
Nathan Everett. 13.
Nathan H., 69.
Nathan Haskall, 69.
Nathaniel, 5, 6, 7, 13, 14, 17, 33, 35, 36, 53, 60, 74.
Newton, 25.

O

Obediah, 76.
Olive Jane, 73.
Orlando II., 13.
Orus, 57.
Oscar Amasa, 74.
Osmer C., 74.
Otis, 63.

P

Paine, 68.
Palmer, 58, 59, 72.
Parker Green, 28.
Parmelia, 18.
Paschal, 63.
Patience Emma, 43.
Paul, 51.
Perry, 67.
Peter, 51, 55.
Pharinda, 62.
Phebe, 24, 42, 51, 55, 57, 62, 68.
Phebe A., 44.
Phebe Ann, 48.
Philip, 38, 39, 63.
Philura M., 74.
Phyletha F., 62.
Polly, 16, 36, 57, 61.

R

R. Almont, 61.
Rachel, 21, 59.
Randal Bartlett, 62.
Rebecca, 6, 19, 31, 36, 39, 54, 55.
Reginald Heber, 39.
Reuben, 11, 23, 43.
Reuben Hill, 23.
Rhoda, 9, 15, 17, 43, 57.
Rhoda B., 68.
Rhoda Jane, 13, 14.
Rhoda Rosette, 18.
Richard, 2, 3, 5, 6, 9, 10, 12, 13, 14, 16, 17, 18, 77.
Richard H., 39.
Richard Peaslee, 16.

Robert, 1, 2, 3, 5, 42, 50, 51, 52, 53, 57, 59, 61, 68, 69.
Robert B., 68.
Robert C., 69.
Roselette Jane, 20.
Rosella, 75.
Rosella C., 73.
Roswell, 54, 63.
Roswell F., 64.
Roxilana, 56.
Rufus, 57, 68..
Rufus II., 69.
Russel, 73.
Ruth, 8, 31, 36, 51.
Ruth Annie, 19.
Ruth Augusta, 71.
Ruth Emily, 15.
Ruth Lane, 26.

S

Sabrina, 26.
Salem Grant, 63.
Sally, 11, 13, 14, 16, 17, 22, 38, 45, 56, 61, 62.
Sally A., 65.
Sally Luann, 62.
Sally M., 64.
Sally Maria, 45.
Salome, 20.
Samuel, 4, 11, 24, 35, 51, 54, 58, 61, 76, 77.
Samuel A., 61.
Samuel Currier, 9.
Samuel Eaton, 40.
Samuel Houston, 16.
Samuel L., 61.
Sarah, 3, 4, 5, 7, 9, 10 14, 15, 18, 24, 27, 31, 32, 33, 35, 40, 42, 44, 51, 52, 53, 54, 56, 57, 60, 71.
Sarah A., 73.
Sarah Adams, 14.
Sarah Alice, 18.
Sarah Ann, 13, 14, 20, 39.
Sarah E., 18.
Sarah Elisabeth, 22, 24.
Sarah Gilbert, 65.
Sarah Jane, 22, 40, 70.
Sarah Josephine, 29.
Sarah Lorraine, 71.
Sarah Luann, 62.
Sarah Lucy, 69.
Sarah Maria, 73.
Sarah Minerva, 71.
Sarah Rachel, 37.
Sarah T., 27.
Sarah Tilton, 30.
Serecta A., 74.
Serecta R., 74.

Sereno W., 67.
Seth Otis, 62.
Silas, 52, 59, 72.
Silas Ariosto, 72.
Simeon, 76, 77.
Simeon Philip, 77.
Simon, 76.
Solomon, 43.
Sophia, 22, 36, 45, 56, 57, 72, 73
Sophronia, 36.
Stearns A., 74.
Stephen, 43, 46.
Stephen Burt, 20.
Stephen Warren, 18.
Sumner, 58, 71.
Susan, 25, 26, 28, 39, 43, 77
Susan Catherine, 43.
Susan Emily, 18.
Susan Henderson, 66.
Susanna, 20.
Sylvanus, 56.
Sylvester, 44.
Sylvester W., 44.

T

Tamah, 51.
Tirza, 56, 66.
Tirza L., 65.
Thomas, 4, 46.
Thomas Bucklin, 48.
Thomas Fisher, 43.
Thomas Jefferson, 18.
Thomas Knowlton, 46.
Thomas Worthen, 9, 10, 18.
Tryphrey, 62.

V

Vernelia, 71.
Vernon, 67.

W

Walter, 52, 56, 67.
Walter Edgar, 72.
Walter Fairfield, 67.
Walter Scott, 39.
Ward, 6.
Warren Colburn, 28.
Warren Jacob, 18.
Welcome W., 62.
Wilbur, 67.
Wilfred Lincoln, 26.
Willard Cooke, 23.
William, 17, 34, 35, 36, 38, 39, 40, 44, 70, 71.
William C., 44.
William Dunbar, 48.
William Ebenezer, 72,
William Ernest, 40.
William F., 36.
William Francis, 63.
William Garland, 24.
William Henry, 26, 40
William Hill, 44.
William Hook, 29.
William James, 43.
William Lewis, 63, 65.
Willie, 48.
Willie Amos, 24.
Willie Burt, 20.
Willie E., 61.
Willie Francis, 72.
Winfield Scott, 73.
Woodbury, 77.

Z

Zadock, 55
Zebina, 65.

NAMES OF COLLATERAL FAMILIES.

A

Abbott, 13, 17.
Achus, 42.
Adams, 14, 56, 57, 72.
Albee, 61.
Alden, 48, 61.
Aldrich, 58, 64, 65.
Allen, 5, 37, 61.
Ames, 46.
Appleton, 18.
Arnold, 62.
Atwood, 62.
Austin, 66.
Avery, 16.

B

Bacon, 73.
Bagley, 9, 19.
Bailey, 62.
Baker, 3, 5, 37.
Balcom, 59, 72.
Ball, 57.
Ballard, 48.
Bangs, 57, 69.
Bardwell, 15.
Barnard, 15.
Barnes, 1, 66.
Baron, 9.
Bartlett, 28, 30, 36, 48.
Beadle, 4, 76.
Bean, 21, 40, 72.
Belden, 44.
Belknap, 54, 62.
Bickford, 38.
Bingham, 60.
Birdley, 2.
Birthrong, 73.
Bishop, 53, 61.
Blake, 38.
Blanchard, 13, 40, 56.
Bliss, 45.
Blood, 28, 64, 72.
Boardman, 32, 33.
Bosworth, 32.
Bourne, 48.
Boyington, 29, 30.
Boynton, 63.
Brackett, 77.
Bradley, 49.
Bradstreat, 36.
Braman, 44.
Brickett, 34.

Brooks, 71, 73.
Brown, 4, 6, 7, 15, 24, 27, 37, 40, 65.
Bryant, 16, 17.
Buck, 61.
Bucklin, 46, 47.
Bullard, 13.
Burkley, 61.
Burlingame, 73.
Burnham, 44, 73, 74.
Burrill, 56.
Burroughs, 24.
Bursiel, 20.
Buswell, 27.
Butler, 43.

C

Califf, 13.
Campbell, 34.
Capron, 18, 46.
Carlisle, 45.
Carlton, 17.
Carpenter, 17, 43.
Carr, 60.
Carter, 24.
Case, 44, 48, 61.
Cass, 11, 20.
Chadwick, 26.
Chaffee, 43.
Chandler, 31, 68.
Chase, 13, 26, 29.
Cheney, 16.
Chick, 18.
Chickering, 54.
Choat, 4.
Chute, 76.
Clark, 60, 63, 66, 73, 74.
Clemens, 63.
Clement, 36.
Clifford, 10, 18, 20.
Clough, 14.
Cluly, 40.
Coburn, 28, 59.
Colby, 13, 28.
Collins, 8, 28, 30.
Colvert, 63.
Conant, 45.
Cook, 45, 48, 52, 60.
Corlen, 65.
Corlis, 27.
Courser, 13.
Cowden, 44.
Cox, 63.
Cozens, 56, 67.

Crocker, 48.
Crofut, 14.
Crosby, 62.
Cross, 38, 42.
Cudworth, 56.
Cummings, 25, 51, 73.
Currier, 8, 9, 14, 15, 16, 19, 20, 22.
Curtis, 44.
Cushing, 6.
Cutler, 48.
Cutts, 76.

D

Daggett, 58.
Danforth, 13.
Daniels, 62.
Davidson, 70.
Davis, 18, 36, 77.
Day, 36.
Dean, 26, 63.
Dearborn, 6, 20, 26, 27, 28.
Dennis, 48, 49.
DeMerritt, 27.
Demond, 15.
Dike, 50.
Dodge, 27, 60.
Dody, 73.
Donnel, 76.
Dow, 17.
Dowley, 74.
Drake, 20, 62.
Draper, 68.
Dresser, 40, 54, 65.
Dunbar, 54.
Duncan, 73.
Dunster, 61.
Durkee, 16.
Dutch, 33.
Dutton, 22.

E

Eames, 48.
Eastman, 5, 6, 7, 29, 30.
Eaton, 23, 36, 39.
Ellis, 59.
Elwell, 65.
Emerson, 11, 21, 24, 27, 45, 63.
Emery, 64.
Enos, 45.
Estey, 53.
Evans, 7.

F

Fairfield, 52.
Farrar, 61,

Fay, 64, 67.
Fellows, 18.
Field, 69.
Fife, 23.
Fifield, 40.
Flanders, 6, 7, 27.
Flint, 21.
Flye, 70.
Ford, 45.
Foss, 15.
Foster, 51, 77.
Fox, 11.
Franklin, 45.
Freeman, 63,
French, 6, 9, 11, 12, 15, 18, 20, 22, 23, 29, 30.
Fuller, 14, 42, 43.

G

Gale, 20.
Gardner, 62.
George, 14, 15, 16.
Gibbs, 44.
Gibson, 25.
Giddings, 33.
Gilbert, 45.
Gile, 17.
Gill, 8.
Gilmore, 63.
Godfrey, 23, 25.
Goodwin, 16, 19.
Googins, 76, 77.
Gordan, 42.
Goside, 48.
Gould, 34.
Grant, 4.
Gray, 54.
Green, 28, 66.
Griffin, 12.
Griffith, 52.
Griswold, 73.
Grundie, 45.

H

Haddock, 6.
Hale, 32, 61.
Hall, 10, 21, 45, 65.
Hambleton, 74.
Hammond, 74.
Hardy, 40.
Harrington, 65, 73.
Harris, 2, 4.
Harrison, 22.
Hart, 44, 59.
Haseltine, 29.
Haskall, 32, 36.

Haskell, 32, 57, 60.
Hatch, 68.
Hayes, 6.
Haynes, 21.
Hayward, 40.
Heath, 16.
Henderson, 56.
Henry, 45, 68.
Hersey, 27.
Heyward, 59.
Higley, 26.
Hill, 18, 23, 25, 44.
Hillar, 37.
Hills, 11.
Hilton, 30.
Hobbs, 9, 56, 67.
Hodges, 59, 72.
Hodgkins, 4.
Hoit, 37.
Holbrook, 55, 66.
Holman, 50, 53.
Holmes, 28, 62, 77.
Holton, 68.
Hook, 29.
Hopkins, 68.
Hosmer, 67.
Hotchkiss, 48.
Houston, 58, 71.
Hovey, 52.
Howe, 10, 52, 55.
Howland, 62.
Hoyt, 8, 15, 27.
Hubbard, 22.
Hubbell, 45.
Hudson, 58.
Hunt, 8, 24.
Hutchenson, 52.
Hutchinson, 51, 54.
Hutton, 36.

I

Ingalls, 19.

J

Jackman, 6, 8.
Jay, 67.
Jenks, 13, 69.
Jennison, 71.
Jewell, 16.
Jewett, 16, 23, 72.
Johnson, 21, 60, 62, 66, 70, 74, 76.
Jones, 7, 31.
Judkins, 12, 27.

K

Keith, 58.
Kenyon, 61.
Kidder, 74.
Kilburn, 74.
Kimball, 12, 14, 21, 64.
King, 7, 45, 56, 63.
Kinman, 45.
Knight, 55, 68, 72.
Knowls, 23.
Knowlton, 33, 46, 60.

L

Lakeman, 34.
Lamb, 53.
Lane, 14, 23, 24, 25.
Langdon, 62.
Langley, 29.
Larabee, 46.
Larcom, 59.
Larkin, 72.
Larned, 53.
Lathe, 48.
Lawrence, 54.
Laws, 61.
Lazell, 69.
Leavitt, 62.
Leighton, 39.
Lernec, 27.
Leslie, 38.
Lewis, 62.
Lilley, 71.
Little, 50.
Livermore, 56, 66.
Locke, 13, 29, 56.
Loomis, 46.
Lovejoy, 36.
Low, 32.
Lyman, 54, 75.

M

Magoon, 13, 18.
Manahan, 26.
Mann, 55.
Manning, 43.
Mansfield, 60.
March, 31.
Marden, 18.
Marsh, 45.
Marshall, 28.
Masters, 68.
Mattoon, 16.
Mayo, 14, 60.
McCoach, 67.
McIntire, 67.

Meriam, 56, 66.
Merrill, 66.
Mesler, 68.
Messer, 43.
Metcalf, 24.
Milliken, 76.
Miltemore, 34.
Mitchell, 13.
Moore, 18, 46, 69.
More, 44.
Moren, 45.
Morgan, 37.
Morrill, 6, 7, 8, 12, 26.
Morse, 28, 29, 74.
Morton, 44.
Mosely, 46.
Moulton, 13.
Mullet, 67.

N

Nay, 11.
Newell, 74.
Newman, 32, 34.
Newton, 72.
Nichols, 53, 58, 61, 63, 70, 71.
Noyes, 21, 31, 45, 63, 65, 66.
Nutting, 57, 69.
Nye, 39.

O

Opp, 44.
Ordway, 2, 12, 22.

P

Page, 39.
Paine, 49, 68.
Parker, 54.
Patch, 57, 59.
Patten, 22.
Payson, 36.
Peabody, 25, 26.
Pearson, 6.
Peaslee, 16, 17, 19.
Peck, 28.
Penrow, 57, 70.
Perkins, 38.
Perry, 55.
Phelps, 26, 54, 68.
Philips, 68.
Pierce, 60.
Pike, 7, 9, 29, 58.
Pillsbury, 20, 21, 23.
Pinedo, 63.
Pinkham, 37.
Poland, 34, 37.

Pope, 33, 61.
Powell, 17.
Pratt, 13, 56.
Presho, 55.
Prince, 23.
Pristol, 58, 71.
Pruden, 78.
Purington, 14.
Putnam, 33, 51, 58, 67, 70.

Q

Quimby, 7, 9, 21.

R

Radford, 37.
Ramsdell, 53, 60.
Randall, 21.
Redman, 56.
Rhodes, 43.
Rice, 69, 74.
Rich, 52, 58.
Richards, 35, 43, 49.
Richardson, 20.
Riggs, 36.
Robie, 27.
Robinson, 74.
Rogers, 18, 36.
Rollins, 27.
Ross, 3, 48.
Rounds, 37, 70.
Rowell, 18.
Russell, 28.

S

Safford, 33, 37.
Salisbury, 39, 40, 48.
Sanborn, 12.
Sanborne, 9, 14, 15.
Sanderson, 57, 68.
Sargent, 16.
Savery, 52.
Sawyer, 7, 12, 14, 16, 37.
Scribner, 9.
Seaver, 58.
Seavy, 22.
Seeben, 68.
Severance, 4.
Shackford, 27.
Shaw, 26.
Shelton, 45.
Shepard, 27.
Sheppard, 61.
Sherwin, 31, 32.
Sholes, 59.
Short, 37.

Shumway, 70, 71.
Sibley, 50, 51, 70.
Slade, 43.
Smith, 22, 23, 32, 39, 42, 43, 47, 48, 65.
Smyth, 25.
Souther, 33, 36.
Southwick, 73.
Southworth, 50, 66.
Sparhawk, 46.
Spinney, 27.
Standard, 68.
Stanton, 45.
Stark, 17.
Stearns, 54.
Stevens, 8, 13, 17, 28, 58, 67, 70, 73.
Stewart, 37.
Stickney, 34, 37.
Stockwell, 54, 56.
Stoddard, 66.
Stone, 38, 50, 65.
Sylvester, 62.
Symonds, 2. .

T

Tabor, 28.
Taylor, 55.
Tenney, 70.
Thayer, 54. 62.
Thompson, 2, 17, 48.
Thorley, 31.
Thorne, 5.
Thurston, 9, 17.
Tibbetts, 13.
Tilton, 12, 29, 30.
Towle, 24, 37.
Tounsend, 1.
Town, 27, 64.
Towne, 50, 51, 53
Townsend, 1.
Treadwell, 53.
Treat, 44.
Tritner, 48.
True, 29.
Tuck, 25.
Tucker, 40, 43, 62.
Tufts, 13.
Tupper, 45.
Tuttle, 77.
Twiss, 59, 67.
Twichell, 74.

V

Van Horn, 28.
Vassall, 66.

W

Wade, 14.
Waite, 66.
Walker, 14, 66.
Walsh, 36.
Walton, 6.
Ward, 60, 63, 64, 74,
Warren, 39.
Waters, 45.
Webster, 6, 29.
Weeks, 13.
Wells, 44.
Wesson, 67.
West, 18.
Weston, 27.
Wetherell, 54.
Wheat, 22.
Wheaton, 27.
Wheeler, 46, 64.
Whitaker, 47.
Whitcomb, 54.
White, 34, 44, 55, 60, 61.
Whiting, 44, 52, 57.
Whitney, 71, 72.
Whittemore, 54.
Wicker, 66.
Wilcox, 44.
Wiley, 71.
Willard, 51.
Williams, 25.
Williston, 43.
Wilson, 64.
Withington, 62.
Witiam, 52.
Wood, 4, 57, 61, 69.
Woodbury, 63.
Woodman, 18, 25.
Woodruff, 46.
Woods, 14.
Worthen, 9.
Wright, 69.
Wyman, 16.

Y

York, 41.
Young, 52, 59.